THE BOOK OF LISTS

FOOTBALL

Stephen Foster's account of a season following Stoke City, *She Stood There Laughing*, was one of the best-selling sports books of 2004. He lives a stone's throw from Carrow Road, home of Norwich City FC, the only English team to have beaten Bayern Munich at the Olympic Stadium, winning a UEFA cup tie 2–1 in 1993.

THE BOOK OF LISTS
FOOTBALL

compiled by
Stephen Foster

CANONGATE
Edinburgh · New York · Melbourne

First published in Great Britain in 2006 by
Canongate Books Ltd, 14 High Street,
Edinburgh, EH1 1TE

1

Copyright © Stephen Foster, 2006

British Library Cataloguing-in-Publication Data
A catalogue record for this book is available on request from the
British Library

1 84195 761 5 (10-digit ISBN)
978 184195 761 6 (13-digit ISBN)

Designed by Tony Lyons
Typeset by Sharon McTeir, Creative Publishing Services

Printed in Great Britain by Clays Ltd, St Ives plc

www.canongate.net

ACKNOWLEDGEMENTS

AB, Albatross, Andysith, Awag, Basilrobbiereborn, Becks, Belly, Bernoulli, Bo, Brispie, Bromley, CaptainSambuca, Catfry, Coxy, Daley_Lama, Denby, Grover, Hoopy, Herts Seasider, IdleParapsych, Jerichoharris, Leonie, Mandy, Moordown, Gymgirl, Michelotti, MikR, Moordown, Moz, Murphy's-Headgear, Njjk, North Stand-Nellie, Northstokie, OldStokie, Orangeish, Paddy, Pear, Penelope Pitstop, Plan Bee, Richard, S43Owl, Sideshow, Turtletiger, Wizaard.

SOURCES

Many websites were visited while putting this book together. I'm indebted to the following which were particularly useful, diverting, and entertaining:

bbc.co.uk/sport; barnsleyfc.org.uk; blackpoolreferees. co.uk; concacaf.com englandfootballonline.com; fifa. com; fiveaside.net; football365.com; footballanorak.com; football.guardian.co.uk; goalkeepersaredifferent.com; holmesdale.net; hurryupharry.bloghouse.net; homepage. eircom.net; laughtc.co.uk; nationalfootballmuseum. com; nobok.co.uk; observer.co.uk; premierleague.com; saintsforever.com; soccerbase.com; sport.telegraph. co.uk; timesonline.co.uk; uefa.com; uglyfootballers.com, wikipedia.org.

Phil Shaw's *The Book of Football Quotations* (Ebury Press, 2003) was also a useful reference guide.

PERMISSIONS ACKNOWLEDGEMENTS
(INTERNAL IMAGES)

Danny Blanchflower © Manchester Evening News; José Mourinho, Diego Maradona, Birgit Prinz, Abel Xavier, Lev Yashin, Johan Cruyff, Pele, Fabien Barthez, Eric Cantona, Hull City Players, Taribo West, Jürgen Klinsmann: all © Action Images; David Beckham, Socrates, Vespa, Juventus badge, Tom Finney, Nou Camp Stadium: all © EMPICS; Playpic shadowgram © EMSOA, reproduced with permission from *Referee* magazine; Aerial image of Dundee and Dundee United stadiums © Royal Commission on the Ancient and Historical Monuments of Scotland / Licensed via www.scran.ac.uk; Wagonwheel © www.nicecupofteaandasitdown.com; Jimmy Glass cartoon © Elmo; Harry Redknapp © Sports Photos; 1930 World Cup football © National Football Museum; Subbuteo figures © www.tablesoccer.net; Wayne Rooney, Football Terraces, Bobby Moore: all © Getty Images; Harry the Haddock © Grimsby Town FC

For Johnny Neptune

CONTENTS

INTRODUCTION

Football is life. Our teams are as familiar and significant to us as our families, but the matches in which they play last for only ninety minutes once or twice a week. This leaves about 7500 hours a year in which we must find ways to occupy ourselves. We watch the rest of the world play football of course, form loose allegiances, anti-support our enemies, and sometimes go outside for a kick-about of our own. But there is still much time left over, a void that is filled by words.

The listing of statistics and the memorising of facts can be seen as the basic grammar of football – it is a necessary badge of honour to have at instant recall the knowledge that Shrewsbury Town play at The Gay Meadow, even though you have never been there yourself, or that Dave Challinor holds the record for the longest recorded throw-in, even though you have never personally seen him demonstrate this rare talent. But beyond the detail lies a more lurid world. The length of Challinor's best throw is 50 yards; to counteract this threat, during a League game, Barnsley removed the towels that he used for drying the ball, shifted the perimeter hoardings closer to the pitch, and had their substitutes warm up in such a way as to hinder his run-up. This is the detail I love, the who did what, the who said what, to whom, when, where, how and why, and in what extravagant choice of words; this is the stuff that keeps me going when the football itself is generally unwatchable. The rumour and speculation, the anticipation and analysis, the ludicrous episode, the improbable anecdote: this is the daily bread of football, and it is all this that this collection celebrates.

And it celebrates in the choicest of language. When the lexicon is remodelled and retooled in the mouth of the inspired practitioner – *Samassi Abou don't speak the English too good* (Harry Redknapp) – the talk that accompanies the game can become as beautiful and ugly as the action itself. To hear a chairman say, 'I'm not going to drag it out or make a point, because points are pointless', is to understand why you remain addicted to the sport. It is because the chairman has brightened your day, confirmed your opinion of him (that he is barking), and handed you on a plate an expression you may utilise in future to irritate your loved one – *I'd like to make a point darling, but I won't, because points are pointless. And while I'm at it – not making a point – did you know, incidentally, that Harry the Haddock, the Grimsby Town inflatable mascot, was actually a rainbow trout?*

The organising formation used in *The Book of Lists: Football* echoes the classifications used in *Roget's Thesaurus*. As I was searching the Thesaurus soon after being asked to compile this edition, it became apparent to me how readily the list of categories in that invaluable work lent themselves to football. This is for a simple reason: the classifications in Roget are arranged by emotional and intellectual indicators – Feelings, Values & Ideals, Behaviour, The Mind and Ideas – in short, the self and the senses: it's through these basic receptors that football infects the being of its followers. 'Some people think football is a matter of life and death. I am disappointed with that attitude. I can assure you it's much, much more important than that.' I've heard it said that Bill Shankly's famous quote was tongue-in-cheek; personally, I doubt it.

Like football, *Roget's Thesaurus* is a work which concerns itself with substitutions and displacements – a world in which one word offers a shade of meaning of another until it gives way to a different interpretation altogether. To use Roget is to search for the *mot juste*, to find the seagull that follows the trawler, via the eternal elusive signifier, the word. As it says in another well-known book, 'In the beginning was the word.' But pretty soon after the word a pair of rolled-up socks and two trees were being used for a game of shooting-in, and afterwards, the first ever post-match discussion was conducted over the original post-match pint.

While players and systems change, the game remains the same; much as it is about competition, spectacle or sometimes even entertainment, at its heart it's about communication. There are those – and I number myself amongst them – who prefer to spend time with Jeff Stelling and his panel of experts on Sky *talking* about fixtures in progress, rather than flicking over and watching the actual stuff itself on another channel. The hours that are devoted to opinion before, during and after the match are as much a part of the action as the action itself, very often more so.

Enhanced by contributions from distinguished writers including Trezza Azzopardi, Stuart Cosgrove, Magnus Eriksson and George Szirtes, and including many entries and suggestions from fans around the world, *The Book of Lists: Football* collects the best of all the talk, stats, incidents and opinions without which football would be just a game.

THE BODY AND THE SENSES

IT'S A PHYSICAL *AND* A MENTAL GAME, MY SON

WORLD IN MOTION
By **Trezza Azzopardi**

10 APHORISMS
PAIN – 16 SICKNOTES
PAIN II – THE 'KEEPER'S CUT
RSI (TROUSERDOG'S TOP 10 ADE AKINBIYI MISSES)
A DOZEN CAUTIONS
BAD HAIR DAY – 10 SUICIDE BLONDS
10 COMPROMISING POSITIONS

WORLD IN MOTION
novelist **Trezza Azzopardi** kicks things off

The Japanese have a single word – *senzuri* – for male masturbation (literally, and maybe in some cases, optimistically, it means 'one hundred rubs'), and they even have one word to denote a woman who appears attractive from behind, but not from the front. She is *bakku-shan*. But I've yet to find, in any language, a single word to describe the athlete who looks divine in motion and distinctly unattractive when they stop still. They come from all sporting arenas. There's the tennis player, who, sweating and stretching and bending from the waist seems to fulfil your heart's desire; and so you wait, unusually interested, for the post-match interview, only to find that, freshly laundered and under the studio lights, he – or she – shines more like a buttered potato than a jewel, and, more to the point, looks like one. In the case of footballers, it shouldn't be important; anyone who's seen Ginola smirking out from their Sunday supplement could argue that, not only do looks not matter to the game, sometimes they positively get in the way. But there's no sensation to lift the sensual spirits higher than the sight of Ryan Giggs running down the wing like a rat in an alley, or Ray Parlour, transformed from ginger mop-top to demi-god simply by the act of movement and that magic ingredient, sweat. Body-builders know this, and porn models know this: action + sudation = sensuality.

The beautiful game never used to interest me in this way. In the time before I became a football fanatic's partner,

I lived on the margins of football awareness; I'd enjoy watching the World Cup, or the European Championships, but my enjoyment was as fleeting as the England team's chances. They looked like nice, healthy lads, they did a fair bit of running up and down; sometimes, they scored a goal. Then the flags that had adorned windows, rooftops and car aerials would gradually disappear, at least until the next round of international patriotism. I thought I understood enough, pre-football-fanatic-partner, to see the attraction of the game, but didn't know a sweeper from a striker, and whether it was a diamond or a 4–4–2 made no difference to what I was seeing. Direct or indirect, it was the *kicking* of the free kick I liked, along with the running, and the jostling, the occasional blood, and the inevitable sweat.

If there was any clue to my burgeoning fetish, it was Euro '96. I was in a small town in France, supervising a group of students at a film festival. While the other groups watched art cinema in the dappled evening light, the British contingent headed off in search of a dark bar showing a live match. Sometimes, this involved sitting in the proprietor's back living-room with his ancient mother, who would feed and water the whole party before settling down with us to enjoy the football on her little telly in the far corner. Often, the café owner would usher us into an unused room – the cellar, or the shed; once, a man with a bar the size of a postage stamp wheeled the television out onto the pavement. We were never refused if it was at all possible. With such hospitality on offer, I should have committed my adultery against England with the French team. But love is fickle, especially if the initial attraction is physical: I fell for Italy. It was completely shallow: they gave good kit, they were a *tiny* bit dirty, they ambled round the pitch like they were strolling down the Via Condotti on a Saturday night, and when no one expected it, they filched the odd goal. There was Maldini, Dino Baggio, Albertini. They looked good moving, and were nothing to write home about when they didn't (which was a lot of the time), except for Maldini, whose thousand-mile stare revealed the aspect of a psychopath contemplating his next bout of torture. Italy were out after the first round, and took my heart with them. It wasn't just their insouciant conduct that got me snared (and removed them from the competition); watching Italy play was like sitting ringside at Smackdown with a catalogue of the Sistine Chapel open on your lap.

I've tried to find other clubs – in Britain – which offer that kind of motile beauty. I got close with Man U, a quarrel of uglies if ever there was one, but over time the likes of Cantona retired and Stam got vanished, and they took on new, pretty blood: Ronaldo, who tip-toes over the pitch like a girl on the dancefloor looking for her earring; and that young hairdresser's assistant, Alan Smith. I'm confined these days to seeking out individual players for merit in the I-love-you-running-but-not-in-a-million-years-standing-still stakes, and have yet to find the perfect word to describe them. *Tamaya!* perhaps, will have to do. It's a Japanese exclamation for viewing that rare thing – a sensual, visceral delight, which dissipates the moment it stops – a firework in the night sky.

10
APHORISMS

Danny Blanchflower
(c. 1954–57)

THE great fallacy is that the game is first and last about winning. It's nothing of the kind. The game is about glory. It's about doing things in style, with a flourish, about going out and beating the other lot, not waiting for them to die of boredom.

Danny Blanchflower, captain of the Tottenham Hotspur team which became the first English side of the twentieth century to achieve the League and FA Cup double, in 1961.

2. Other countries have their history. Uruguay has its football.
   Ondino Viera, *manager of Uruguay's 1966 World Cup team.*

3. If this can be termed the century of the common man, then soccer, of all sports, is surely his game. In a world haunted by the hydrogen and napalm bombs, the football field is a place where sanity and hope are still left unmolested.
   Sir Stanley Rous, *6th President of FIFA, speaking in 1952.*

4. Without the ball, you can't win.
   Johan Cruyff, *legend. Along with Michel Platini, Cruyff is the only other player to win three European Footballer of the Year awards.*

5. A penalty is a cowardly way to score.
   Pele, *legend. Holder of the world record for professional hat-tricks (92), and for the number of goals scored at international level (97).*

6. Every defeat is a victory in itself.
   Francisco Maturana, *Colombian coach.*

7. Norway beat Brazil who beat Chile who drew with Italy who beat Norway. Therefore clearly Norway are a much better side than Norway.
   Steve Jones, *Internet reporter at World Cup '98, explaining how football actually works.*

8. Winning the World Cup is the most beautiful thing to have happened to France since the Revolution.
   Emmanuel Petit, *French international footballer, '98.*

9. We don't have any splits here. The players' country is Liverpool Football Club and their language is football. **Gerard Houllier,** *as manager at Anfield.*

10. Sometimes in football you have to score goals. **Thierry Henry,** *giving expert advice: in October 2005 Henry surpassed Ian Wright's record to become Arsenal's all time top scorer, reaching 186 goals at the age of 28.*

PAIN – 16 SICKNOTES

1. Keith O'Neill

Fans of Norwich City, Middlesbrough and, most especially, Coventry City, will tell you that Keith O'Neill deserves a hospital ward to be named in his honour. Bringing his 'playing' career to a conclusion at Coventry, the Republic of Ireland winger broke his hand on a *punch bag* at the training ground while recovering from a foot injury that came on the back of a double leg fracture that he acquired in his initial comeback training session. The comeback training session was after a back injury which followed on from a hip injury which followed on from a groin injury. When he finally made his first team reappearance in August 2003 (some 18 months after the original back injury) he lasted just seven minutes before he was injured, and substituted for one last time as a professional footballer.

2. Svein Grondalen

The Norway defender had to withdraw from an international during the 1970s after colliding with a moose while out jogging.

3. **Milan Rapaic**

The Croatian marauder missed the beginning of Hajduk Split's 1995/96 season after he accidentally poked himself in the eye with his boarding pass when he was at the airport in Split.

4. **Charlie George**

Arsenal's 1971 FA Cup hero managed to cut off his toe with a lawnmower.

5. **Rio Ferdinand**

During his time at Leeds United, the England defender picked up a strain while watching television. Ferdinand had his foot up on a coffee table for a number of hours which flared-up a tendon behind his knee.

6. **Alan Wright**

The diminutive former Aston Villa full-back strained his knee by stretching to reach the accelerator in his new Ferrari. He subsequently swapped the performance vehicle for a Rover 416.

7. **Steve Morrow**

The Arsenal and Northern Ireland defender broke his collarbone after falling off the shoulders of Tony Adams while celebrating the 1993 League Cup Final win against Sheffield Wednesday.

8. **Lee Hodges**

Barnet player Hodges slipped on a bar of soap in the shower and wrenched his groin.

9. **Alan Mullery**

The Tottenham and England star missed the 1964 tour

of South America after injuring his back while brushing his teeth.

10. **David Batty**

Former Leeds, Blackburn and England midfielder managed to re-injure an Achilles tendon when he was run over by his toddler on a tricycle.

11. **Darren Barnard**

The Barnsley midfielder was sidelined for five months with a torn knee ligament after he slipped in a puddle of his puppy's urine on the kitchen floor.

12. **Elena Marcelino**

The player with a girl's name was apt to cry off with a cold sore or a little nick from shaving (his legs). Being injured was the natural state of the Spanish centre-half whom Ruud Gullit bought for Newcastle United from Real Mallorca for a mere £5.8m in 1999. Scans on the affected areas were often declared to be inconclusive. On one occasion a very nasty injured finger kept him out for months on end. By then there was no shortage in Tyneside of fans who would happily have given him two fingers.

13. **Two fans**

The *British Medical Journal* of September 1996 reported that Alan Shearer's opening goal for England against Germany in the Euro '96 semi-final was vigorously celebrated throughout the country by football supporters. An accompanying X-ray plate showed two broken bones – a bicondylar fracture of the tibial plateau, and a fracture of the calcaneum – which occurred as two armchair supporters, aged 36 and 54, celebrated

Shearer's header with the customary jumping up and down in front of their television set. The journal went on to suggest that this sort of injury might be prevented by a pre-match warm-up and use of the correct footwear (i.e. not slippers).

14. Sexually acquired reactive arthritis

In 1999 the *New Scientist* reported on research into this condition, which causes inflammation (redness, swelling, pain) in different parts of the body at the same time, or in different parts of the body at different times. The research found that it especially afflicts footballers. It seems they have so much sex that they're a high risk group for SARA, which in turn makes them unusually susceptible to on-pitch injuries to, for example, the knees.

15. Perry Groves

On the bench at Arsenal, Groves jumped up to celebrate a goal, hit his head on the roof of the dug-out, knocked himself out and needed treatment for concussion.

16. Ramalho

The Brazilian star managed to put himself in bed for three days after swallowing a suppository intended to treat a dental infection.

PAIN II – THE 'KEEPER'S CUT

Can it be only coincidence that the clumsiest men in football tend to apply for the job that gives them the maximum opportunity to demonstrate their clumsiness?

1. **Alex Stepney**

   In 1975 the Manchester United goalkeeper Alex Stepney dislocated his jaw while shouting at his defenders during a match against Birmingham. (Former England midfielder Brian Greenhoff replaced Stepney between the sticks and kept a clean sheet.)

2. **Chris Woods**

   David Seaman won his third England cap in 1989 as a result of an injury sustained by first-choice goalie Woods, who cut his finger open after wrestling with the string on his tracksuit bottoms with a penknife.

3. **David Seaman**

   Missed the first half of the 1996/97 season after damaging his knee ligaments by bending down to pick up his television remote control. He went on to almost end his career by injuring his shoulder while trying to land a big carp.

4. **Mart Poom**

   The Estonian 'keeper missed some pre-season training during his time at Derby County after injuring his genitals in a charity match against an Iron Maiden XI.

5. **Kasey Keller**

   The American international knocked out his front teeth in 1998 while pulling his golf clubs out of the boot of his car.

6. Richard Wright

Everton's custodian faced a spell on the sidelines after damaging his shoulder by falling out of his loft hatch as he was trying to pack away his holiday suitcases in 2003. Developing a reputation as something of a virtuoso in this category, in February 2006 Wright injured his ankle by falling over a sign placed in the goalmouth during the warm-up of an FA Cup replay at Chelsea. The sign read: NOT IN USE – PLEASE PRACTISE IN TEMPORARY GOALMOUTH.

7. Vince Bartram

Buy one, get one free: Gillingham's Bartram broke his wrist in a league game against Millwall at the start of the 2003/04 season: the injury was inflicted by his opposite number, Lions 'keeper Tony Warner, who collided with Bartram after coming up for a last-minute corner.

8. Chic Brodie

The Brentford 'keeper's career came to an abrupt end in October 1970 when he collided with a sheepdog that had run onto the pitch. While the dog got the ball, Brodie shattered his kneecap. In summing up the unfortunate incident, Chic said, 'The dog might have been a small one, but it just happened to be a very solid one.'

9. Dave Beasant

The veteran goalkeeper managed to rule himself out for eight weeks in 1993 when he dropped a bottle of salad cream on his foot, severing the tendon in his big toe. Of course he did: you drop the Heinz, seconds later you've severed a tendon. It could happen to anyone.

10. **Santiago Canizares**

Spain's goalkeeper missed the 2002 World Cup after accidentally shattering a bottle of aftershave in his hotel sink. A piece of glass fell on his foot, severing the tendon in his big toe. Of course he did: you drop your Lynx, seconds later you've severed a tendon. It could happen to anyone.

11. **Andy Dibble**

Welsh international Dibble suffered severe chest burns from sliding along a field in 1999 when he was playing for Barry Town against Carmarthen. Dibble, who had to have a skin graft, believed it was chemicals on the field that caused the burns. Ouch.

12. **Aiden Davison**

The Grimsby 'keeper was felled by an egg during a Second Division play-off game against Fulham in 1998. But it *was* a hard-boiled egg.

RSI

A special category for Hackney-born Nigerian international Ade Akinbiyi. We're not picking on him, and he does score goals sometimes, which is a very hard job. But Ade's repetitive strain syndrome is one that provokes a knock-on complaint in supporters: repeated banging of the head against the wall. He's played for clubs too numerous to mention, but Stoke City fan Trouserdog speaks for many in the following compilation of highlights from Akinbiyi's 2003/04 efforts.

Trouserdog's Top 10 Ade Akinbiyi Misses

Ade (indicated), unmarked and clean through, prepares himself to receive the ball, close his eyes and hit it at the 'keeper ...

1. **vs Leeds** when he was clean through but closed his eyes and hit it at the 'keeper.

2. **vs Coventry** when he was clean through but closed his eyes and hit it at the 'keeper.

3. **vs Burnley** when he was clean through but closed his eyes and hit it at the 'keeper.

4. **vs Crewe** when he was clean through but closed his eyes and hit it at the 'keeper.

5. **vs Wigan** when he was clean through but closed his eyes and hit it at the 'keeper.

6. **vs Ipswich** when he was clean through but closed his eyes and hit it at the 'keeper.

7. **vs Preston** when he was clean through but closed his eyes and hit it at the 'keeper.

8. **vs Leicester** when he was clean through but closed his eyes and hit it at the 'keeper.

9. **vs Derby** when he was clean through but closed his eyes and hit it at the 'keeper.

10. **vs Millwall** when he was clean through but closed his eyes and hit it at the 'keeper.

A DOZEN CAUTIONS

'There's no rapport with referees these days. If you say anything you get booked, and if you don't they send you off for dumb insolence.' Jack Charlton, 1983

1. **For building a snowman**

   During his time as the country's best amateur goalie at Bishop Auckland, former Blackpool 'keeper *Harry Sharratt* (who was reserve for the 1953 FA Cup Final against Bolton) was booked for rolling a snowman on his goal line during a match played on Boxing Day. Sharratt was also reported to have spent idle moments during uneventful, one-sided games surveying the action from the top of his cross-bar.

   Still, he might be more mobile than Fatty Foulke. (*See* Lard XI, p.103)

2. **For having one sock up and one sock down**

   According to the rulebook, 'shinguards must be worn on the field of play, and they must be covered entirely by the stockings' (socks to you and me). *Steve Claridge,* of very many clubs, routinely goes about Pippi Longstockingstyle. Mr Pedant from Penge, refereeing at Brentford one afternoon, once bothered to caution him for this.

3. For having a laugh

One of *Paul Gascoigne*'s many sidelines included taking the Mickey out of refs; for instance on the occasion when he sniffed an official's armpit while he was holding his hand high to signal a free kick. Undeterred by the frosty reception that his pranks usually earned him, throughout his career Gazza continued to test his theory that bastards can have a sense of humour. When the referee dropped his card during a Rangers vs Hibs game, Gazza picked it up and mock yellow-carded him. Naturally, he was booked for his troubles.

4. For celebrating too enthusiastically

Italian *Enzo Maresca* saw yellow before ever stepping on the field for West Bromwich Albion. He was pulled up for the offence of displaying joy while still on the sub's bench (actually, a portion of him, his leg, was on the pitch, which was probably where he made his fatal mistake).

5. For piping a tune

Birmingham City were playing Chester in a League match and were 3–0 up. With a few minutes to go, *Liam Daish*, their captain, headed home a fourth. In the following celebrations some Birmingham fans threw a toy trumpet onto the pitch. Daish picked up the instrument and started to play it. The booking which followed led to a three-match ban.

6. **For being a First Aider**

    In a fixture between Leicester and Coventry in the Premiership in 1999 Leicester were playing dreadfully and a flag-happy linesman was making it worse. At one point there was a collision on the touchline between a couple of players, and the linesman was injured as a result. Leicester player *Neil Lennon* went off the pitch into the disabled spectator area and got an empty wheelchair for him. Such an example of good citizenship certainly merits the booking that was Lennon's reward for his helpful attitude.

7. **For ironic applause**

    Gary McAllister was an early exponent of this popular form of misbehaviour, gaining himself a mere booking when captain of Coventry during a match of many sendings-off-for-nothing at the Britannia Stadium in 2003.

8. **For being a babe**

    David Beckham received his third sending-off for Real Madrid in October 2005, also, nominally at least, for ironic applause. A teammate offered a different interpretation. 'Maybe it's because he is blond and pretty, referees are capable of sending him off for that', said Uruguayan hard man Pablo Garcia. Maybe. Or perhaps it was because of his developing reputation: earlier in the same month Beckham had been ordered from the field for a second yellow card in a World Cup qualifier against Austria, thus becoming the first England player to be sent off twice, as well as the first England captain ever to be dismissed.

9. **For a bad combination**

Tommy Burns was sent off for Celtic *after* he'd been substituted. As he left the pitch he hurled some abuse at the referee, shook hands with the sub and made for the tunnel. The official called him back and issued a yellow card, his second of the match. Although this meant an automatic dismissal, Celtic were allowed to continue with 11 men because the substitution had taken place before the sending off.

10. **For someone – or possibly someone else – saying something or another**

In the 1978 World Cup group game between Holland and Germany, the referee appeared to send off *René Van Der Kerkhoff*. The player was already going down the tunnel when the ref sent an official to pull him back, because the player he actually intended sending off was *Dirk Nanninga*. The offence was foul and abusive language: Nanninga insisted he'd only asked if they could just get on with the game following a stoppage. The referee later admitted he didn't understand what Nanninga had said, but whatever it was, he knew it wasn't nice.

11. **For a tactical discussion**

In a Dr Marten's League Eastern Division match between Eastleigh and Rothwell Town, *Nicky Banger* was sent off with ten minutes to go when, in answer to shouted instructions from his manager from 80 yards across the field, he responded with some industrial language. Whatever message the gaffer was trying to convey, it was unlikely to have been, 'Get yourself f***ed off for an early bath, sunshine.'

12. **For kicking an old bag**

Blackburn gaffer *Mark Hughes* was sent to the stands for this heinous crime during a match at Stamford Bridge in 2005.

BAD HAIR DAY – 10 SUICIDE BLONDS (AND 1 HONOURABLE MENTION)

You only have to look at the career of David Beckham's locks to know that footballers have too much time on their hands. When they're not choosing between trays of platinum diamond ear studs in Aspreys or getting a new tattoo they're to be found under the celebrity hairdryer at Vidal Sassoon. But it's when they let the girlfriend loose with the peroxide bottle that things go seriously kinky afro in a rub-a-dub stylee.

1. **David James**

(England and many clubs, noted particularly for his speed, acceleration and his dyed hair.) Blond Harpo Marx on six-foot-four-accident-prone goalie; not a great idea, and a much worse look. Prompted fans to chant, 'There's only one David Gower' at him. And as for the elaborate experiments with facial landing strips, let's not go there, as they say.

2. **Colin Hendry**

(Scotland and many clubs, noted particularly for his speed, acceleration and his dyed hair.) Natural blond, but a Scot: only a ginger barnet works for our Caledonian cousins. Dry-flyaway problems to boot, problems only exacerbated by a fluffy mullet.

3. **Carlos Valderrama**

   (Columbia and many clubs, noted particularly for his speed, acceleration and his ...) Well, *he* says it's natural, but then he would, wouldn't he? Even Barbra Streisand would think twice before indulging in a three-foot wide strawberry perm.

4. **Djibril Cissé**

   (France and many hairdressers, noted particularly for his speed, acceleration and his dyed hair.) David James with knobs, beads, extensions and topiary. Cissé has a hairdresser in France who designs his hair every few weeks. This person once designed it red. Cissé learned a lot from:

5. **Abel Xavier**

There goes Zeus

   (Portugal and lots of clubs, noted particularly for his speed, acceleration and his dyed hair.) Pioneer of the peroxide beard. 'There goes Xavier, who looks just like Zeus, not that I have any idea what Zeus looks like ...' as BBC radio commentator Alan Green once remarked.

6. **Ibrahim Ba**

(France and all over the place.) The skilled midfielder came up through Bordeaux and was bought by Silvio Berlusconi for AC Milan in '97 for a fee exceeding €12 million in order to add some ill-advised close-cropped blond glamour to the Lombardia region. Ba's career eventually saw him wash up at Swedish side Djurgården. On signing him, the Djurgården head coach Kjell Jonevret commented, 'I must say I was a bit sceptical. But according to what we have seen so far the signing is a fantastic stroke for us.' Fans tend to find that, like fish and houseguests, Ba soon goes off, but many before Jonevret have been deceived by his flashy blond ways, including managers at Le Havre, Perugia, Olympique Marseille, Bolton Wanderers and Çaykur Rizespor of Turkey.

7. **Barry Venison**

(England, Sunderland, Liverpool, Newcastle United, Galatasaray, Southampton etc.) Achieved notoriety for wearing heinous shiny suits in combination with the mother of all blond northern mullets to achieve a look that even Peter Stringfellow might have considered a bit vulgar. *Barry stat*: was the youngest ever captain of a League Cup final side when he led Sunderland out at Wembley in 1985 at the age of 20 years and 220 days.

8. **Robbie Fowler**

(England, Liverpool, Leeds, Man City, Liverpool etc.) It was for a mercifully brief period, which is the best you can say about it. Looked like the consequence of a prank his mates had perpetrated by experimenting with sulpher dioxide in a biology lesson. As an indicator of how scary it was: you cannot find an image of it on the internet with *safe search* on. *Robbie stat*: holds the record for the fastest Premiership hat-trick – 4 minutes 32 seconds against Arsenal in 1994.

9. **Paul Gascoigne**

(England, Newcastle, Spurs, Lazio, Rangers, Middlesbrough, Everton, Burnley, Boston United, Kettering Town etc.) Gazza is legendary for a lot of stuff including dyeing his hair five times in one day because he was bored, and the questionable decision to go with a blond Catweazle goatee while on a book tour.

10. **David Beckham**

The man himself. Lost a little of his pace, and some of his blondness. Corn rows, Alice bands, the 'Jesus look' – whatever it is that's wrong with young people today, most of it is Beckham's fault. You only had to see the barmy army of tiny tots 'larging it' in the playground while sporting bottle-blond Mohawks during World Cup 2002 to know that.

1 **Honourable Mention**

XI Wrong Blonds – The Romanian team at France '98.
When they went down for the huddle prior to the kick-off of their final group game it created a total white-out. Was this full-squad platinum dye supposed to intimidate the opposition? Sadly it just gave Hagi & Co the aspect of an All-Star Chavs XI. They drew 1–1 with Tunisia (it takes more than a rotten barnet to scare a Tunisian) and exited the tournament, shorn of all dignity.

10 COMPROMISING POSITIONS

1. **The Kosher**

   Politicians demanded an inquiry into reports that the Israeli national team spent the night with prostitutes before suffering a humiliating mauling in the European Championships qualifying play-offs in 1999. Israel suffered an 8–0 aggregate defeat at the hands of Denmark, but the tie was effectively over after they lost the home leg 5–0. Following the game, there were newspaper allegations that the players had partied like it was 1999, having prostitutes called to the team hotel in Tel Aviv. National coach Shlomo Scharf helped pour oil onto troubled waters by saying that while he was looking into the matter it was possible that the hotel staff quoted in the papers had actually seen players' wives and girlfriends rather than girls of the night. Israeli Internal Security Minister Shlomo Ben-Ami offered a government analysis: that the Danish team was so much better than Israel that the result would have been the same if it had been *their* players who spent the night with call girls. *The Kosher,* and its variant *El La Manga,* is the alleged preferred position of most teams on tour.

2. **The Doc**

   There are any number of alleged players, coaches and managers who allegedly had to resign because they allegedly had it off with another staff member's other half.

3. **The Roast**

   In this position the alleged incident will take place in a luxury suite of a five-star hotel. There will not be a banquet of suckling animal; instead there will be a team of famous sportsmen, two young vestal virgins, and several front-page exclusives the following morning.

4. **The Tanya**

In this position raunchy simulations of alleged roasting incidents are video-taped and secretly distributed in popular dramas like *Footballers'Wives*.

5. **The Wheelbarrow**

For the advanced practitioner; here a 19-year-old 'glamour model' sleeps with a footballer and the morning after goes to see a PR man to find out whether she might have become famous. The PR man asks, 'Was he married?' The glamour model says 'Yes' (Or 'No', it makes little difference). The PR man phones a tabloid editor and in a final consummation of the act of love the glamour model gives birth to a barrow load of the money shot. (Sometimes known as *the mercenary position*.)

6. **Doggy Style**

Most comfortable for the retired footballer. Here the 'receiver' watches couples have sex – dogging – in their cars in softly-lit multi-storey car parks. The receiver can reverse his position to become a 'giver' by confessing his sins to a tabloid newspaper. In selling his tale of shame and debauchery to the press for the small matter of a five-figure sum he will once more become a receiver; in this way he can achieve deep market penetration and enhanced satisfaction.

7. **The Sven**

Apparently lacking passion on the job in public life, those who indulge in *the Sven* have tendencies to enjoy the company of a small harem of ladies in private, and secretly are as steamy as a sauna.

8. **The Brazilian**

In the '70s, when João Saldanha was coach of 'the Canarinha', Pele's swinging teammates faced just a single tough rule: only one girl each per week. Saldanha's advice was simple: 'Look, you can go with girls, it's natural. I only ask one thing: never change the girl during the week, only on Mondays. Sleep with a girl twice a week, that's normal. But if you change the woman, then it's problems – emotional ones.' When a goalkeeper transgressed the code by attempting to switch his date in midweek, Saldanha stepped in and confiscated her.

9. **The Anal**

In which the chairman of a football club sells all the best players and gives the supporters a proper shafting. This popular position is also known as *Business as usual*.

10. **Going Down**

Scientists have measured data that records a 20 per cent decrease in testosterone levels in fans following a defeat for their team, and a converse rise for the winners. The advice seems to be, if you want to stay up, win.

FEELINGS

IT'S BEEN EMOTIONAL

DOWN THE LANE AND THROUGH THE MILL
By **Anjali Pratap**

JOY – 15 CELEBRATIONS

A SENSE OF LONELINESS
AND FAILURE – 12 SWIFT P45s

ISOLATION

CONTEMPT – 12 NOT ENTIRELY
SPORTING COMMENTS

IRRITATION, ANNOYANCE, TEDIUM, DESPAIR
AND ENNUI – 12 GOALLESS DRAWS

WRETCHEDNESS – 10 EXCEPTIONALLY POOR
GOALS-IN-A-SEASON TALLIES

FALLING WITH STYLE: THE WORST
LEAGUE RECORD EVER

INEVITABILITY, MONOTONY, PLUS ÇA CHANGE …

DOWN THE LANE AND THROUGH THE MILL

with new-born fan and literary agent,
Anjali Pratap

When I'm at White Hart Lane, I stick out like a sore thumb. There are plenty of females there, but they don't seem to shout like I do. I'm small and have a middle-class accent which blends in in some places, but not at a football ground (unless it's Highbury or Stamford Bridge). I'm like Eliza Doolittle yelling, 'Move your bloomin' arse' amongst the toffs with my reedy Surrey accent, shouting 'Oh come *on* you Spurs'. But no matter how out of place, all inhibition goes and I can't help blurting it out. This makes watching a match more or less hell. We avoid the family stand at White Hart Lane, such is my foul and vocal disgust when Spurs are not doing well. People seem to think it's hilarious, a stream of obscenities coming out of a petite, well-spoken woman. But football has not turned me into someone else; I'm either high or low and nothing in between – I've come to realise that the unrestrained anger is just me being more me than usual.

To make matters worse, having had a mid-twenties conversion to football, I have the fanaticism and ignorance of the convert. Though, I very soon got over the feeling of happy expectation at the beginning of a game we 'should' win, I think maybe, like a child, I take the knocks harder than the seasoned fan because I'm still in the process of acquiring the weary cynicism.

The wrench that football puts on my emotions is best encapsulated in three games I saw in quick succession in the 03/04 season. The first was the fairytale. We were at the bottom of the table. It was the opening match of the New Year and we knew we had to go and give our love. It was cold and dark but we were upbeat in the way that you are when things simply cannot get any worse. It was the first time I'd sat at an end, with people who shout louder than I do, and I've never looked back. The whole pitch was laid out before me like a massive snooker table. Birmingham were sixth and looking really good. The first half passed like a dream as goal after goal (three) went in for us. I have difficulty remembering whether I've been so happy since. The second half was more hairy, but still nothing took away from how everyone must have felt leaving the match; amused, bemused and proud that our team – leaky old Spurs as we were before Paul Robinson was around and Ledley King really came into his own – could have shown such spirit. I want to cry just thinking about it.

Which made the experience of the FA Cup replay at home to Manchester City all the more horrific. This tie followed Birmingham, and we sat in almost the same seats. The first half seemed practically identical to the Birmingham game in its joyousness, the same three goals and the added bonus of them having Nicolas Sulky Anelka sulking off the pitch, and City's Joey Barton getting sent off just for *saying something*. Perhaps I wasn't the only one guilty of the jinxing sin of half-time smugness. Because what came after was pure punishment. When ten-man City equalised to 3–3 near the end I was staring straight into a footballing *Heart of Darkness*. Their winner just before the final whistle seemed impossible in the way that death feels impossible in the young. I wasn't watching by then. I wish I could have adopted the stoicism of my boyfriend who at least had the good grace to be impressed and grimly awestruck at what had happened. I was just looking at the floor, dry mouthed with grief and disgust and I saw that plenty of other people felt the same way. I do think I was grieving, crass as that sounds.

My anger increased for the next game, against Portsmouth. I would have chosen not to go, only we'd bought the tickets in advance. Another 4–3 scoreline, another gamut of emotions. I continued where I'd left off, I simply couldn't look at the team to start with, I was white-hot with anger. Angry people are worse when they go silent and detached. Thinking about it now I was behaving in much the same way as I do when I'm furious with my boyfriend for some supposed misdemeanour. The detachment feels very serious and even scares *me* (I feel like I'll never come back from it), but really it only takes a few Ferrero Rochers to bring me round. Spurs handed out the chocolates with what now seems like an utterly ridiculous win in which we kept scoring and they kept equalizing: 1–0, 1–1, 2–1, 2–2, 3–2. The moment of rallying was when Pompey fans chanted, '*4–3, we're gonna win 4–3*' when it became 3–3. I was so hyped up that by the time we got the final goal in I *started* the same chant at the North End in retaliation. So I got my Ferrero Rochers, but why does it always have to be this way – the gift always an apology. Why can't they just present me with a bunch of flowers, gratuitously, sometimes? Other teams' fans seem to get a bouquet out of the blue from time to time, don't they?

JOY
-15 CELEBRATIONS

Maximum points for artistic interpretation

BRYLCREEM®, side-partings, good manners and the half-time fag have gone the same way as the modest wave to the fans. Back in the old days your teammates would shake your hand, or, if it was an absolute howitzer, may even have gone so far as to pat you on the back once you've been good enough to satisfy your job description by finding the back of the net. Then came the snogging of the '70s, the breakthrough moment that paved the way for what we see today, a situation in which celebrating the moment has gained equal prominence with the moment itself. (Don't try some of these at home, not unless you want to be certain to look a tit.)

1. **The Dying Swan**

   Jürgen Klinsmann joined Tottenham Hotspur in 1994 following performances in successive World Cup tournaments – Italia '90 and USA '94 – during which his fame as the Diver's Diver reached global proportions, nowhere more so than in England where supporters are on permanent red alert for skulduggery from Ze Germans. Klinsmann scored his first goal for Spurs away at Sheffield Wednesday; in an inspired choreographed gesture, which won over a significant amount of the non-partisan, he celebrated by running to the touchline and performing a self-mocking cartoon bellyflop, just ahead of his teammates, who all followed suit.

2. **Tooting a Line**

   Amid tabloid allegations of cocaine abuse, *Robbie Fowler*, of Liverpool, had spent his afternoon on the receiving end of taunts from Everton fans during a Merseyside derby. After scoring from the penalty spot Fowler celebrated by kneeling down and crawling along the touchline, pretending to snort it. To keep him sweet, the FA issued him a six-match ban.

3. **The Dog's**

   José Antonio Reyes scored and was piled on by teammates who bundled him to the floor while one teammate very obviously bit his *cojones*. Apparently this incident is based on an old Spanish proverb which translates as, 'You are so good that I will eat your nuts.' *That*, at least, is the explanation *Guillem Balague*, the nut muncher, gave to TV reporters who were curious about his part in the celebration.

4. **The Havana**

In the '80s, when Liverpool were an all-conquering force both at home and in Europe, the only solace Manchester United fans could take was that Liverpool always struggled against their team. These were the circumstances that inspired *Gordon Strachan* to stand in front of Liverpool fans simulating smoking a fine Cuban cigar before his United teammates put an end to the embarrassing charade by mobbing the Caledonian ginger poppet.

5. **The 'Pas de Problème'**

As finessed by *Thierry Henry*: scores, shrugs, looks a bit bored, puts finger to lips to quieten the cheering. Some see this as magnificent insouciance, others think, 'what a tosser'.

6. **The Olga Korbut**

Nigeria's *Julius Agahowa* received the line of 9.9s and one perfect ten from the Olympic judges after performing six successive somersaults following his opening goal against Sweden in the 2002 World Cup. Honourable mentions also go to widely travelled winger *Peter Beagrie*, who brought the playground cartwheel to football, and to the ever-athletic Congolese international *Lomana LuaLua*. Following a consistent goalscoring run for Portsmouth, one bookie was offering this special bet:

If LuaLua scores against Arsenal how many somersaults will he do?

> 1–3 5/2
> 4–6 9/2
> 7–9 50/1

7. Rocking the Baby

Brazilian star *Bebeto* broke the deadlock in the crunch game against Holland during the 1994 World Cup in the USA. With *Rai* and *Romario* joining on either side of him and duplicating the move he celebrated the recent birth of his child by running to the touchline and making the shape of a cradle with his arms, which he rocked gently from side to side. An instant maternity-ward classic, like all the best celebrations its currency has spread far and wide – one report suggests it was even seen replicated during a match between Cardiff City and Brighton and Hove Albion, which must at least have enlivened matters.

8. Milking It

It helps to be Gallic

As perfected by *Eric Cantona* when he scored that sublime chip against Sunderland. The genius is in the arrogance: jutting, nodding, circling in the round, chin up, chest out, hands on hips, collar upturned, lapping it up. It helps to be Gallic.

9. Dirty Dancing

Instigated by *Roger Milla* during Italia '90 when he did the *Makossa* – the rhythmic step-forward dance made popular in the Cameroonian city of Douala – with the corner flag. Milla spawned a million imitators, and one specialist:

10. Lee Sharpe sings Elvis

Once one of the most coveted wingers in England, winning trophies with Manchester United, *Sharpe* skimmed down one wing while *Ryan Giggs* flew down the other. The Birmingham-born wide man also went a long way to proving that the King is indeed alive and well. His celebration involved approaching the nearest corner flag at speed and then using it as a microphone where, complete with strained expression and dramatic bend of the knees, he would treat his public to a quick rendition of 'Hound Dog'.

11. The Temuri Ketsbaia

Not acrobatic or difficult to re-create, the Georgian international became a cult hero for Newcastle United after scoring a vital goal against Bolton and then proceeding to rip his shirt off and boot the stuffing out of the advertising boards while shoving his teammates away. He would later say he had been 'Happy, no angry', and profess to wonder what all the fuss was about.

12. The Aylesbury Duck

Rymans League side Aylesbury United came to popular attention in 1995. Aylesbury went on an FA Cup run and reached the third round. This achievement would probably have faded away into memory had their players not performed a choreographed West End chorus line in celebration (of losing 4–0); the team formed an orderly line, got down on their knees and waddled along the Loftus Road pitch like a paddling of ducks, much to the bemusement of the QPR supporters.

13. The Drunken Auntie at a Wedding

Cameroonian whizz kid *Samuel Eto'o* celebrated Barcelona's League title in 2005 by shouting, 'Madrid, you arseholes, salute the Champions!' He shouted it six times into a microphone, in front of 100,000 people in the stadium, not to mention all the world's media. 'I'm sorry,' Eto'o apologised the next day. 'I have spat on the plate that used to feed me.' Eto'o is, of course, an ex-Real player.

14. The Cockroach

Real Madrid's Brazilian stars *Ronaldo*, *Robinho* and *Roberto Carlos* rolled on their backs and wiggled their arms and legs in the air during a win over Alaves. Spanish teammate Helguera gave Roberto Carlos a kick for his efforts, saying it was disrespectful to the opposition. Alaves president Dmitry Piterman called the players 'clowns' and 'spoilt kids' for their behaviour. Spain's Anti-Violence Commission called on the football federation to charge Piterman for his 'outburst'. This is what happens when you have a Commission.

15. The Boys' Brigade Clown

With his unusual gift for doing exactly the wrong thing at exactly the wrong time, Paul Gascoigne chose to celebrate his first goal for Rangers in 1995 (against Celtic) by miming playing a flute as he pranced along the goal line. Flute-playing, traditionally associated with Protestant marching bands, is not admired by Celtic's largely Catholic supporters and Gazza was accused of inflaming sectarian passions. He was so chastened that he waited nearly three years before doing the very same mime while warming up to go on as a substitute in another Rangers v. Celtic match, for which he was fined two weeks' wages.

A SENSE OF LONELINESS AND FAILURE – 12 SWIFT P45s

'It's an impossible job; everyone thinks they can do it better than you, and the only certainty is getting sacked.' Sir Bobby Robson

1. **Bill Lambton**

   Was 'in charge' at Scunthorpe for **three** days in April 1989. Though he never signed a contract, he did at least get to be manager for one game, a 3–0 defeat to Huddersfield. To hear Jack Charlton's view, it is hard to imagine how Lambton lasted even that long. Charlton, who played under Lambton at Leeds, recalled him as an ex-army fitness fanatic, but not as a coach in football. 'One day he told us that anyone worth his salt ought to be able to kick the ball in his bare feet and never feel it, so one of the lads said to him, "Well, go on, then". He finished up hobbling off with all of us laughing at him. A few weeks later the chairman asked if we wanted the manager to leave – and every one of the players said yes. Bill said, "If you let me stay, we'll have a new start", but nobody said a dicky bird. He was sacked that same day.'

2. **Dave Bassett**

Moved from Wimbledon to Crystal Palace in May, 1984, but after a mere **four** days, and before he'd signed a contract, he found himself out on his arris. Or changed his mind, depending on which version you prefer.

3. **Kevin Cullis**

In 1996 Swansea City appointed Cullis, whose previous experience amounted to running a team in the Cradles Heath Youth League. Cullis's friend, Michael Thompson, 'bought' The Swans (the deal never went through) and gave his mate the hot seat. Cullis selected the team for a couple of games before the pros at the club revolted and forced him out: apparently, due to a completely blank look on the face of 'the manager', Swans midfielder David Penney was forced to give the half-time team talk in the second, and final, match of the Cullis-era which lasted **seven** days. As a postscript, Cullis was sentenced to nine months in jail in 2003 for fraud.

4. **Mickey Adams**

In a textbook case of the time-honoured 'promised funds never materialised' routine so beloved of football chairmen, Mickey Adams – later to prove himself an adept manager at Leicester City – lasted an unlucky **thirteen** days, plus three unlucky defeats out of three, when he took the post at – once again – Swansea City, in October, 1997.

5. **José Camacho**

In the summer of 1998, having been hired by Real Madrid president Lorenzo Sanz, Camacho swiftly fell out with the top man. There were rows over a contract for fitness trainer Carlos Lorenzana, and then over Sanz's involvement in player affairs. Just **twenty-three** days after arriving at the Bernabeu, Camacho was out on his ear without taking charge of a single match. He did a little better on his return to the position in 2004, lasting a full 115 days before taking his second bullet.

6. **Tommy Docherty**

The Doc's **twenty-eight** days at Queens Park Rangers in December 1968 began with chairman Jim Gregory making money promises. Docherty wanted to buy a player from Rotherham, for £20,000 or so, Gregory didn't want to, so Docherty left, with something of a non-sequitur for a parting shot: that QPR were the un-fittest team he'd ever seen. He did considerably better, time-wise, in his next post, surviving thirteen months as the first of many managers appointed by notorious hire 'em, fire 'em henchman 'Deadly' Doug Ellis at Aston Villa.

7. **Steve Coppell**

At the end of a successful spell with Crystal Palace, Steve Coppell's reign at the club ended in relegation from the Premiership at the end of the 1994/95 season, albeit with 49 points – the highest-ever total for a relegated top division club. After a break from football and some coaching work back at Palace, Coppell returned to management, agreeing a three-year deal at Manchester City on 7th October 1996. On 8th November the same year, **thirty-two** days later, he resigned on medical advice, thus becoming the most short-lived manager in the club's history. The pressure of the job had 'completely overwhelmed' him and made him ill. He appeared at a news conference with chairman Francis Lee to say, 'I'm not ashamed to admit that I have suffered for some time from huge pressure I have imposed upon myself … to such an extent that I cannot function in the job the way I would like to. As this situation is affecting my well-being, I have asked Francis Lee to relieve me of my obligation to manage the club, on medical advice. I am therefore resigning for personal reasons. I'm extremely embarrassed by the situation and I would like to apologise first and foremost to Francis Lee and his board, who have done everything in their power to help me.'

Fortunately for Steve, he made a miraculous recovery, and four months later at the end of February 1997, was re-appointed as Crystal Palace manager, looking none the worse for his Maine Road experience. He is still in management, currently enjoying great success with Reading.

8. **Steve Claridge**

Millwall sacked the striker for whom the term 'journeyman' was invented, after just **thirty-six** days in the summer of 2005 following some sort of contretemps (that no one was ever able to get to the bottom of) with recently returned ex-chairman Theo Paphitis. Claridge's record read: played four – two wins, a draw and a defeat – all friendlies.

9. **Paul Gascoigne**

It was already beyond most fans to be surprised by anything Gazza got up to in his life, but all the same it came as slightly unexpected news when he became co-owner and manager of Conference North side

Kettering Town late in 2005. Much more predictable was the length of the reign: **thirty-nine** days plus thirty-seven verbal warnings from chairman Imraan Ladak concerning alleged incidents involving alcohol.

10. **Brian Clough**

Having delivered the League Championship to Derby County in 1972 Clough arrived at Leeds United in 1974 in a whirlwind of publicity and big-mouthedness which did not go down well with the reigning League Champions, many of whom had been hoping that their long-serving player Johnny Giles would have been offered the chance to take over from Don Revie. Notwithstanding Clough's track record, many Leeds fans regarded his appointment as inexplicable. He was surely Leeds' most outspoken critic (which was saying something of that widely reviled, overtly physical team), and his method of attempting to win over the players went something like, 'Chuck all the medals you've won into the bin, young men, as they weren't won fairly.' His reign lasted **forty-four** days.

11. **David Platt**

Platt resigned as Sampdoria's coach in 1998 after just **forty-eight** days. The former England midfielder had had enough after three defeats, three draws and no victories, while having to listen to rival managers complaining that his coaching qualifications were not up to scratch. His Italian coaching stint was most remarkable for the brave decision to introduce the Elvis-impersonating Lee Sharpe to Serie A. Returning to England in 1999, Platt was appointed player-manager at Nottingham Forest, where he plunged the club deep into debt by splashing out millions on a series of poor signings. Platt left Forest in 2001 and took over the England Under-21 side with moderate success.

12. Luigi del Neri

As Porto basked in the afterglow of their Champions League victory, del Neri was presented to the world as José Mourinho's successor on 4th June 2004. But trouble lay ahead almost immediately for the Italian who had made his name as a miracle-worker with Chievo, the provincial Serie A club. In his attempts to teach his new squad the tactical schemes that had served him so well at his previous team, he was to find that the European Champions did not take kindly to being forced to watch videos of obscure players at Chievo, and soon complained to Jorge Nuno Pinto Da Costa, the chairman. By August 9th, **sixty-five** days after his appointment, Del Nero had been dumped by Da Costa, ostensibly for poor time-keeping: an extended three-day absence from training being the final straw. In the Italian press, Del Neri vowed to claim all the money that he was entitled to from the dismissal. He said that his removal was a result of Porto's fear of change after previous coach Mourinho's success over the last two seasons. (The Special One's boots prove difficult to fill: Del Neri's successor, Spaniard Victor Fernández, lasted just over six months.)

ISOLATION

There are some weird, messed-up people out there who just don't get it. Many of these are commonly known as Americans.

1. Football tournaments are like black holes: even if you don't watch them, you know something's afootie, because everything else is distorted by its gravitational pull. The best way to appreciate football on television is to walk down a city street when a big game is on and listen to the synchronised roars coming out of the buildings over the empty pavement. It gives you a very strong sense of alienation, of not being invited, of being alone.
   AA Gill, television critic, The Times.

2. There are just two things about the World Cup that prevent Americans from caring: it involves soccer, and the rest of the world. When I hear that Tunisia is playing Belgium for the crucial Group H runner-up spot, all I want is a map. The only way Americans are going to learn another country's name is if it attacks us.
   Joel Stein, 'The Rest-of-the-World Cup'
   article in Time Magazine.

3. All that proves is that most of the world is too poor to build bowling alleys, golf courses, tennis courts and baseball fields. There's hundreds of millions of poor people out there who still ain't got indoor plumbing, but that don't mean there's something great about an outhouse. Soccer is boring. I've never seen a more boring sport.
   Mike Royko, American columnist, writing in 1994, the year that the World Cup Finals were held in the USA.

4. But actual, real, living, breathing, non-green-card Americans? For them, the more pertinent question is, 'What World Cup?' America already has, you see, a World Series. Every run-down diner in Philadelphia and Baltimore has a 'World-famous' cheese-steak sub sandwich. But the World Cup? It has as much traction in this country – if fewer Slovenian drag-queens – than the Eurovision Song Contest. As the rest of the entire world is glued to the telly, the one country with more actual responsibility for the world has no idea what's going on. It's hard not to remember the infamous old newspaper headline, summing up British isolationism in Europe: 'Fog In Channel. Continent Cut Off.' Only the right message this time would be: 'Football On Television. America In Orbit Around Planet Earth.'
Andrew Sullivan, Sunday Times, *June 2002*.

5. The rest of the world loves soccer. Surely we must be missing something. Uh, isn't that what the Russians told us about Communism? There's a good reason why you don't care about soccer – it's because you are an American and hating soccer is more American than mom's apple pie, driving a pick-up and spending Saturday afternoon channel-surfing with the remote control.
Tom Weir, USA Today.

6. I misidentified the metrosexual David Beckham as 'captain of Britain's soccer team'. Ain't no such team. Beckham heads England's squad; Scotland, Wales and Northern Ireland all have separate teams. Show me that red tab.
Journalist **William Safire** *runs an apology in the* New York Times Magazine.

7. No football team will win this tournament. This tournament will be won by the faceless empires of corporate greed. The Jules Rimet trophy has become hijacked by the world of big business bastards, sold to the TV networks of Satan. There will be a final on July 12th. It will have no soul. It will be between Nike and Snickers.

   Ireland's RTE's post-match team come over all Eeyore-ish during World Cup '98.

8. Up to five goals is journalism. After that, it becomes statistics.

   A French reporter gives up after Sweden thrash Cuba 8–0 at the 1938 World Cup.

And then there are some smart Alecs who do get it, and mock it all at the same time:

9. This will be, by some measures, the most popular international festival in human history. Television and other media have made the World Cup the mark that the Olympic Games were for the ancient world. Much of the tribal enthusiasm, as it was for the Olympic Games, is patriotic, if not chauvinist. From its beginning more than two centuries ago, *The Times* has risen far above such narrow nationalism. We are the oldest international paper of record. We support underdogs and justice. We look forward to enjoying the magic of such footballing stars as M Zidane and Señor Veron. We shall enjoy the Viking defence of Sweden and the Latin fire of Argentina.

   There is more to football than winning. England invented the beautiful game. It is beautiful because it can be played by anybody on a street or a beach with improvised equipment. It combines the beauty of the ballet with the courage of battle and the miracle of grace under stress.

We cheer for surprises from such underdogs as China and Saudi Arabia. We admire the statesmanship of FIFA in sharing the World Cup between two such hostile neighbours as Japan and South Korea. We look forward to triumph and disaster, surprise and certainty, temperament and stoicism, and to a celebration of sport that extends far beyond local loyalties. May the best side win, and may that side be England.

Editorial in The Times *(of London), 2002*

10. Serie B: never a dull moment, except during the ninety minutes of the match.

From The Miracle of Castel Di Sangro, *by Joe*
McGinniss

CONTEMPT – 12 NOT ENTIRELY SPORTING COMMENTS

1. Francis could not spot a great footballer if the bloke's name had four letters, started with 'P' and ended with 'e'.

Alan Hudson, *'70s maverick talent, on the newly appointed Birmingham City manager, Trevor Francis, 1997.*

2. The most educated person at Real Madrid is the woman who cleans the toilets.

Joan Gaspart, *Barcelona vice president, helping keeping the entente cordiale in 1997.*

3. If brains were chocolate, he wouldn't have enough to fill a Smartie.
   Alan Birchenall, former player, and Leicester City PR officer, sums up 'lovable rogue' Robbie Savage in 2000.

4. Three years at Port Vale is enough for anybody.
   Lee Mills, the former Bradford City striker, clocking off in the Potteries in 1998.

5. The referee is available for Christmas pantomime or cabaret.
   Keith Valle, the Bristol Rovers Tannoy announcer, getting himself into hot water as the players leave the field after a match against Wigan in 1989.

6. I have no interest in Pulis or what he does with his life. For me, he was the most evil, vindictive and malicious person I have ever met or worked with.

   Available for pantomime

   Paul Scally, chairman of Gillingham, welcomes ex-manager Tony Pulis back to Priestfield in his programme notes in 2003.

7. I've told the players we need to win – so that I can have the cash to buy some new ones.
   Chris Turner, Peterborough manager, using reverse psychology (possibly) prior to a League Cup Quarter Final in 1992.

8. He actually looks a little twat, that Totti.
   Ron Atkinson, *employing terrace talk on air. Big Ron retired from punditry after referring to Marcel Desailly in racist terms in an 'off mic' comment in Monaco in 2003.*

9. Look at these small fry. I could piss on them.
   Eric Cantona *endears himself to sports journalists on a French television chat show in 1995.*

10. I can't believe a Huddersfield player actually meant to do that.
    Paul Jewell, *ex-Bradford City manager, plays to his former constituency for the Sky cameras in 2005 when commenting on a free-kick wonder goal from Huddersfield's Mark Hudson in the derby between Huddersfield and Bradford.*

11. If you put all the German players, except Kahn, in a sack and hit it, you would get someone who deserved it.
    Franz Beckenbauer *assesses Germany's (winning) quarter-final performance against the USA, Korea 2002.*

12. There are two great teams on Merseyside; Liverpool and Liverpool Reserves.
    Bill Shankly.

IRRITATION, ANNOYANCE, TEDIUM, DESPAIR AND ENNUI –12 GOALLESS DRAWS

1. *Blackpool 0 York City 0; Division Two, December 1975*
   The highlight was seeing York run out in a white shirt with a red Y (a V-neck and a single stripe continuing down the middle). (Selected by Blackpool fan *Wizaard*)

2. *Stoke City 0 Preston North End 0; Coca-Cola Championship, Boxing Day 2005*
   There were bad roadworks on the M6, and all that anyone can remember is that both sides kept a clean sheet. And to think, some people missed their Nan's famous Boxing Day dinner for this. (Selected by *Northstokie*.)

3. *Chelsea 0 Hull City 0; Division Two, February 1976*
   Only 8000 dispirited souls huddled together chanting 'Loyal supporters' that cold Wednesday night. But by the end, most wished they weren't. (Selected by Chelsea fan *Stan Rodrigues*.)

4. *Colchester United 0 Huddersfield Town 0; Division One, 2005*
   We played a 3–6–1 formation which soon became 5–4–1. There were two shots in the entire game, almost no goalmouth action, and it's not a short journey from Huddersfield to Colchester either. (Selected by Town fan *AndyM_HTFC*.)

5. *Cambridge United 0 Cardiff City 0; Division Two, December 1999*
   This wasn't a boring game, it didn't lack incident,

it was probably entertaining for the neutral but it crushed the spirit of every Cambridge fan unfortunate enough to be there. Three red cards, all waved in the direction of visiting Cardiff players (who also had eight squad players out with the flu), one penalty given to Cambridge, and yet *no* goals. Nil–nil. Against 8 (eight) men. Try and imagine how terrible that is. Furthermore this was against relegation rivals, this was a match that mattered. A 4–0 win at Ninian Park later in the season, and Cardiff's relegation, should have provided some revenge, but over time that game has faded into history whilst the 0–0 is still a festering sore. Nearly six years later I still cannot believe that we did not win and it rankles my ankles. (Selected by Cambridge fan *Bromley*.)

6. *Plymouth 0 Rochdale 0; Division Three, May 2001*
   Some 0–0 draws can be boring, some can be frenetic, some can be intriguing, but this one was simply totally annoying. Rochdale – 28 years since their one and only promotion ever, having never even made the playoffs in 13 years of trying – needed a win at mid-table Plymouth in the final game of the season. The result made no difference one way or the other to Plymouth. A draw would mean that some Johnny-come-latelys (ie deadly rivals Blackpool), could nick the playoff spot that we had held for the last nine months. With nothing to lose you might have thought that Plymouth would have come out to attempt to entertain their large home attendance and finish the season on a high. They were having none of it, they played 4–5–1, might as well have been 9–0–1 the way they defended. Had I been a Plymouth fan I would

have been embarrassed by my own team. Highlights included Plymouth players feigning injury in the first five minutes, a Plymouth full-back standing on the ball in his own box without moving until a Rochdale forward came to challenge him, followed by the obligatory hoof, and Plymouth's 'keeper taking goal kicks from the left when the ball had gone out on the right, and vice versa. Add in that the Plymouth fans only had one song and that is one game I will always remember for all the wrong reasons. It is odd for a team such as Rochdale to have a pathological hatred of a team such as Plymouth, but the game the following season between the two was rather heated to say the least. (Selected by Rochdale fan *Daley_Lama*.)

7. *Bournemouth 0 Hull City 0; Division Two, sometime in 2002*

The Cherries 'keeper Chris Tardif concusses himself in the first five minutes and midfield player Marcus Browning goes in goal. Hull had so worked themselves up into a pre-match frenzy of 'settling for a point' that they spent 85 minutes refusing to even try to make Browning save the ball. (Selected by Bournemouth fan *Andysith*.)

8. *Bournemouth 0 Hull City 0; (The Nightmare Continues) Division Two, about ten years ago, who cares when it was anyway*

Hull, kitted out in their Pizza Hut table cloth 'green-mini-spots-on-white-background' away kit clearly can't afford to wash them so spend 90 minutes trying not to tackle, or shoot, or do anything else that might get them dirty. Hurrah. (Also selected by Bournemouth fan *Andysith*.)

9. *Liverpool 0 Sunderland 0; Premiership, November 2002*

Losing, as Rudi Völler once said, is a concept as well as a fact. Every Liverpool fan here yesterday, as well as Gérard Houllier and his players, may have been reflecting on that last night. For the second time in six days Liverpool drew a game but came away feeling like losers. Liverpool had 24 attempts on goal to Sunderland's none. They stretched Völler's theoretical definitions to the limit but after 90 perplexing minutes their primary feeling was a familiar sinking one. (Opening of *Michael Walker*'s *Guardian* match report of one of the most one-sided goalless encounters in history, and one that seriously dented Liverpool's title challenge that year too. Liverpool also had ten corners to Sunderland's none.)

10. *Goallesszzzzzzzzz Specialists, Bath City*

The team for insomniacs to follow in 1993/4 season were the Gloucestershire side who played out a record 12 goalless draws in the Conference. Over a 42-game season, that's a goalless game ratio of 28.5 per cent.

11. *Goallessballs*

Sir,

Having heard the so-called sports correspondent on this morning's *Today* programme dismiss last night's Liverpool–Chelsea match as 'a goalless bore', I then received the latest 'Eye' and found you too sounding off against nil–nil football matches ('We were boring first' claims Neasden boss). It may surprise you to learn that such scores are usually brought about by well-organised defences on both sides and are often just as exciting as draws earned by skilful captaincy in first-class cricket, as in the third test this summer.

You remind me of the ignorant American TV people who tried to get the goals enlarged when the World Cup was played there on the assumption that the more goals were scored the more popular it would be. Now, I know you don't LIKE football but you should at least try to understand it.

Yours against dumbing down,
Allan Wilcox

(*Letter to* Private Eye, *2005*)

12. *And Finally*

I think the match was a goalless draw, and on reflection an uneventful one, but it didn't seem important. The football game was clearly just the excuse all these thousands of people had for coming together. The real reasons they were there was to have a laugh, to express their brilliant subconscious poetic talents, share floppy hot dogs and to reinforce their view of the world and, more importantly, of Barnsley. It was wonderful. (*John Nicholson*, Internet correspondent for *Football365.Com*. We think John may be American)

WRETCHEDNESS – 10 EXCEPTIONALLY POOR GOALS-IN-A-SEASON TALLIES

1. Stoke City, Division One, 1984/85 (Relegated) (* see following section)
   24 goals in 42 league matches, a goals-per-game average of 0.6

2. Crewe Alexandra, Division Four, 1981/82
   29 goals in 46 league matches, a goals-per-game average of 0.6

3. Redditch United, Conference, 1979/80.
   26 goals in 38 league matches, a goals-per-game average of 0.7

4. Chester City, Division Two, 1994/95 (Relegated)
   29 goals in 46 league matches, a goals-per-game average of 0.6

5. Cambridge United, Division Two, 1983/84 (Relegated)
   28 goals in 42 league matches, a goals-per-game average of 0.7

6. Chelsea, Division One, 1923/24,
   31 goals in 42 league matches, a goals-per-game average of 0.7

7. Bury, Division One, 1911/12 (Relegated)
   32 goals in 38 league matches, a goals-per-game average of 0.8

8. Manchester United, Division One, 1893/94 (Relegated)
   36 goals in 30 league matches, a goals-per-game average of 0.8

9. Carlisle United, Division Three, 1986/87 (Relegated)
   39 goals in 46 league matches, a goals-per-game average of 0.8

10. Exeter City, Division Three South, 1923/24
    37 goals in 42 league matches, a goals-per-game average of 0.9

(At least there is often a relegation battle going on, which may alleviate any tedium created by the lack of goals, even if it does ultimately exacerbate the wretchedness. Averages rounded up to nearest decimal point.)

FALLING WITH STYLE:
THE WORST LEAGUE RECORD EVER

Long before Buzz Lightyear came up with the concept, in the 1984/85 season Stoke City plummeted out of the top flight of English football with a record that remains unsurpassed in England for a 42-match season. In the poorest set of figures ever assembled by a team in any division of the professional Football League, the Potters did not win once away from home all season, scoring only six times. They conceded a record number of goals (91) suffered the most defeats in a season (31), as well as the most home defeats (15), as well as the fewest goals scored. They had the worst goal difference in all Christendom – minus 67, and the fewest home wins (3). They scored only one goal in ten games after Boxing Day, and lost their final ten matches to be relegated with the lowest points total for a season *ever* (17). This under the new 3 points for a win system. The final tally would have been only 14 under the outgoing rule of 2 points for a win. At the top of the table, Everton amassed 90 points from the 42 games. This difference – 73 points – is the largest difference ever recorded in the top division of English football. Stoke have remained out of the top flight ever since. An influx of Icelandic businessmen have, surprisingly, been unable to return the Potters to the promised land.

INEVITABILITY, MONOTONY, PLUS ÇA CHANGE ...

The Norwegian League Champions from 1992 to 2004 were:

1992	Rosenborg
1993	Rosenborg
1994	Rosenborg
1995	Rosenborg
1996	Rosenborg
1997	Rosenborg
1999	Rosenborg
2000	Rosenborg
2001	Rosenborg
2002	Rosenborg
2003	Rosenborg
2004	Rosenborg

In 2005 Vålerenga, of Oslo, messed with the natural order by coming top. Rosenborg finished mid-table.

PLACE AND CHANGE OF PLACE

HOME AND AWAY

WHY I AM A GLORY-HUNTING MANCHESTER UNITED FAN
By **George Szirtes**

10 FAR-FLUNG MANCHESTER UNITED SUPPORTERS' CLUBS
12 GEOGRAPHY STUDENTS
PREMIERSHIP SOCCEROOS XI
OVERPAID, OVERSEXED AND OVER HERE XI
AFRICAN PLAYERS OF THE YEAR
TAKE ME TO THE HIGH GROUND
2 DOZEN TEAMS WHO CHANGED THEIR NAME

12 TEAMS WHO ARE TOO CLOSE FOR COMFORT
10 WHO CROSSED A GREAT DIVIDE
THE 1 PLAYER TO HAVE PLAYED IN THE MANCHESTER,
MERSEYSIDE AND GLASGOW DERBIES
CITY CITY XI

WHY I AM A GLORY-HUNTING MANCHESTER UNITED FAN

by Norfolk-based Hungarian
poet **George Szirtes**

We arrived in England on 2 December 1956 and by March 1958 I was a Manchester United supporter. No, that is not quite accurate: I wasn't a supporter, nor am I exactly that now, if by supporter we mean joining clubs, travelling, following, buying merchandise and phoning in to 606. I wasn't a supporter, but the team, the idea of the team, began to matter. Readers will probably jump to the conclusion that it was the Munich air crash that decided me, and they wouldn't be exactly wrong. But this goes back further.

My first memory of football is being taken to the Népstadion in Budapest. I was five or six at the time. It was a sunny Sunday afternoon and the big open bowl was full. I think we got two whole matches for our money because not all the Budapest stadiums had yet been rebuilt after the war. Budapest had at least six teams then: the best of them being the army team, Honvéd, which starred Puskás, Kocsis and Czibor (all to play in Spain after the revolution of 1956 that brought us to England). The transfer system was simple for Honvéd: they simply drafted the best players. The stadium was full of noise, and far down below players in heraldic kit were running about. My father's favourite team MTK, blue and white, were playing Ujpesti Dózsa, a team in deep violet shirts.

It's all very romantic and aesthetic really. I wanted the team in the violet shirts to win. Then came November 1956 and we walked across snowy and muddy fields into Austria. An aeroplane whisked us off to England. Came the English language, the English seaside, the English winter, the English maisonette and the London terrace. Came school. Came football in the playground. Came the Munich air-crash.

It was not so much the crash perhaps, as what followed. I hadn't been to a match in England yet (Spurs versus Preston North End was to come), and the names of the dead players meant little to me, but somehow I followed the struggle of Duncan Edwards for life, and kept track of the remnant team as they fought their way through to the Cup Final against Bolton where they were beaten after Lofthouse charged Wood into the net, severely injuring him.

It was perhaps a sense of outraged justice, admiration for recovery from disaster and the vain fight for life that got to me, seeped into me as an idea. I still hadn't seen the team, except perhaps briefly on Pathé News in the cinema. They were names and fates. I tried the sound in my mouth. Man-ches-ter involved familiar Hungarian sounds but U-ni-ted involved diphthongs: Hungarian has no diphthongs. It was a satisfactory element of strangeness mastering them.

Then I started going to matches, first with my dad, then with friends. I did the North London tour of Highbury, White Hart Lane, Stamford Bridge, Craven Cottage, Loftus Road and even spent a melancholy afternoon at Brentford arriving on the terraces three minutes late by which time the only goal of the match had gone in. My dad settled for

Spurs, my closest friend of the time was for Chelsea but the magnet was drawing me ever closer to United. In 1962–3 they were almost relegated and I turned to dad after United lost to Fulham and said: They'll go down, won't they dad. Of course not, he answered.

Then things picked up: I saw Law and Best and Charlton (Charlton became my all time hero) and Billy Foulkes, Shay Brennan, Tony Dunne and all. But never in Manchester. That seems crazy. Why not? Probably because the city of Manchester had very little to do with it for me. Manchester United was not in Manchester (I know City supporters say it's in Salford): it was somewhere inside my person. It made a small but vital extra organ in my body. I was not primarily a social creature in any case: loving United was not about gangs, crowds, tribes, solidarity or geography. It was like being in love with Julie Christie: I did not need to go round to her house with a bus full of fans. Because, like Christie, United were beautiful. They played a high risk game in which beauty mattered, not beauty of a poncey frilly kind but, like Christie's, something sensuous and potentially tragic.

Since then I have had soft spots for the teams playing anywhere near where I lived at the time: Leeds United, Luton, QPR and Norwich City, though Graham Taylor's Watford was hard work for an aesthetic-romantic. But at heart it is Manchester United for me. And not because of the trophies either. I have seen United relegated, seen them play half-cock through most of the '70s and '80s, seen them in utter chaos. I regard the last fifteen years as a bonus, an undreamt-of Golden Age. I love Ferguson. I love his fierceness, his loyalty, his vision. I even love his mistakes, which are rarely the mistakes of small-minded caution. I loved the team of the mid-'90s: G Neville, P Neville, Butt, Scholes, Giggs, Beckham, Cantona and all. I think we miss Beckham more than we admit. Who provided all those wonderful passes for Ruud or Solskaer or Cole? Who does that now?

Of the two words Manchester and United it is the second that matters. I wish the city of Manchester well. I have nothing against City (or Siddy, as United fans refer to it). I have not developed a strong antipathy to other teams except perhaps Wenger's prissy but brilliant Arsenal. Can't stand prissiness, hissy-fits, and that don't-touch-me-I'm-an-artist *hauteur*. I think every team needs one mad but honest thug and we have the great Roy Keane. For now.

Because Keane will shortly go, as will Ferguson, and maybe the golden days will go with them. But United isn't this or that particular team. United is the beautiful passionate instinct that rises from its own ashes. You say it's big business? Tough: all major teams are big business. The business too is incidental. I stand in the bar watching Sky, drinking Jamesons. It isn't Sky or Jamesons that sing in the nerves though. It's a never quite completed myth to which I owe my loyalty, a kind of movement, the idea of how things should be, in red and white and black.

10
FAR-FLUNG MANCHESTER UNITED SUPPORTERS' CLUBS

1. **MANCHESTER** United Supporters' Club of Victoria, Australia

Miles from Melbourne to Old Trafford as the crow flies: 10,550

2. *Singapore and South East Asia Reds*
   Miles from Orange Grove Road to Old Trafford as the crow flies: 6796

3. *Malaysia Reds*
   Miles from Kuala Lumpur to Old Trafford as the crow flies: 6615

4. *Japan Reds*
   Miles from Tokyo to Old Trafford as the crow flies: 5885

5. *South Africa Reds*
   Miles from Johannesburg to Old Trafford as the crow flies: 5770

6. *The Manchester United Supporters' Club of Winnipeg*
   Miles from Winnipeg to Old Trafford as the crow flies: 3772

7. *MUSC Malta (The Oldest Manchester United Supporters' Club in the World)*
   Miles from Valletta to Old Trafford as the falcon flies: 1462

8. *Manchester United vefurinn á Íslandi*
   Miles from Reykjavik to Old Trafford as the crow flies: 1014

9. *Scandinavia Reds*
   Miles from Bergen, Norway, to Old Trafford as the crow flies: 549

10. *Invicta Reds, Manchester United Kent Supporters' Club*
    Miles from Canterbury to Old Trafford as the coach full of gloryhunters drives: 260

12 GEOGRAPHY STUDENTS

Don't let this lot read the map.

1. I'd like to play for an Italian club like Barcelona.
   Mark Draper

2. Where are we in relation to Europe? Not far from Dover.
   Harry Redknapp

3. Leeds is a great club and it's been my home for years, even though I live in Middlesbrough.
   Jonathan Woodgate

4. It was like playing in a foreign country.
   Ian Rush *on his time with Juventus in Italy.*

5. Djimi Traore had to adapt to the English game and he did that by going out on loan to Lens last season.
   Rush *again, keeping it up in his work as a pundit.*

6. Well, I can play in the centre, on the right and occasionally on the left side.
   David Beckham, *when asked if he thought that he was a volatile player.*

7. Borussia Mönchengladbach 5, Borussia Dortmund 1: so Mönchengladbach win the Borussia derby.
   Gary Newbon, *ITV commentator. 'Borussia' in Germany is used like 'United' in England.*

8. Matthew The Netherlands.
   Charlton's **Matt Holland** *gets put through the spellchecker for the* Independent.

9. No one on my sports desk gives a shit about soccer ...
    Someone wrote an article about John Harkes going to
    Sheffield Wednesday and the editor changed it to 'going
    to Sheffield, Wednesday'.
    David Waldstein, New York Post *journalist and soccer
    fan.*

10. Playing with wingers is more effective against European
    sides like Brazil than English sides like Wales.
    Ron Greenwood

11. Barcelona ... a club with a stadium that seats 120,000
    people. And they're all here in Newcastle tonight.
    John Motson, *BBC*

12. The Brazilians were South American, the Ukrainians
    will be more European.
    Gold star and a team point for: ***Phil Neville***

PREMIERSHIP SOCCEROOS XI

Mark Schwarzer
MIDDLESBORO

Lucas Neill
BLACKBURN ROVERS

Stan Lazaridis
BIRMINGHAM CITY

Brett Emerton
BLACKBURN ROVERS

Tony Popovic
CRYSTAL PALACE

Ahmad Elrich
FULHAM

Craig Moore
NEWCASTLE UTD.

Josip Skoko
WIGAN

Tim Cahill
EVERTON

Mark Viduka
MIDDLESBORO

Harry Kewell
LIVERPOOL

OVERPAID, OVERSEXED AND OVER HERE XI

1.	**Tim Howard**	Manchester United
2.	**Brad Friedel**	Blackburn Rovers
3.	**Marcus Hahnemann**	Reading
4.	**Gregg Berhalter**	Crystal Palace
5.	**Cobi Jones**	Coventry City
6.	**Claudio Reyna**	Manchester City
7.	**John Harkes***	Sheffield Wednesday
8.	**Eddie Lewis**	Fulham
9.	**Joe-Max Moore**	Everton
10.	**Brian McBride**	Fulham
11.	**Bobby Convey**	Reading

* *The only American to score in a League Cup Final, for Sheffield Wednesday in a 2–1 defeat to Arsenal in 1993. With that goal Harkes also became the only American ever to score at Wembley Stadium.*

AFRICAN PLAYERS OF THE YEAR

Not a single winner of this accolade (awarded by the Confederation of African Football) played in his home continent at the time of the award.

Year	Player	Nationality	Club
1992	Abédi Pele	Ghana	Olympique Marseille
1993	Rashidi Yekini	Nigeria	Vitória Setúbal
1994	Emmanuel Amunike	Nigeria	Sporting Lisbon

1995	George Weah	Liberia	AC Milan
1996	Nwankwo Kanu	Nigeria	Internazionale
1997	Victor Ikpeba	Nigeria	AS Monaco
1998	Mustapha Hadji	Morocco	Deportivo La Coruña
1999	Nwankwo Kanu	Nigeria	Arsenal
2000	Patrick Mboma	Cameroon	Parma
2001	El Hadji Diouf	Senegal	Lens
2002	El Hadji Diouf	Senegal	Lens / Liverpool
2003	Samuel Eto'o	Cameroon	Real Mallorca
2004	Samuel Eto'o	Cameroon	Real Mallorca/ Barcelona
2005	Samuel Eto'o	Cameroon	Barcelona

TAKE ME TO THE HIGH GROUND

1. *National Stadium* in the Bolivian capital La Paz, a breath-sapping 8500 feet above sea level.

2. *The Arequipa*, Peru, venue for 2004 Copa America games, stands 7910 metres above sea level.

3. *The Azteca Stadium* in Mexico City stands at 7000 feet above sea level.

4. *Silverlands*, home to Buxton FC, which is more than 1000 feet above sea level, is the highest football ground in England.

5. *St James' Park* Newcastle United's ground has seen stand redevelopment which has created the largest cantilever structure in Europe. The capacity is now over 52,000,

of which up to 3000 away fans can be accommodated. As always with away fans, they put you in the worst bit. If you're going to St James' Park, go to the gym first; be warned: you climb 14 flights of stairs up to the Gods.

6. *The Hawthorns* – built in 1900, home of West Bromwich Albion – is the highest League ground in England, standing at 551 feet above sea level. (Next come Vale Park (Port Vale) 525 feet, and Boundary Park (Oldham Athletic), 509 feet.)

2 DOZEN TEAMS WHO CHANGED THEIR NAME

Not all teams have kept the same name – but which name matched which club?

Then		**Now**
1. Dial Square	a	Cambridge United
2. Small Heath Alliance	b	Everton
3. South Shore	c	Bristol Rovers
4. Christ Church FC	d	Arsenal
5. Boscombe St John's	e	Birmingham
6. Black Arabs	f	West Ham United
7. Abbey United	g	Queens Park Rangers
8. Riverside	h	Wolverhampton Wanderers
9. Shaddongate United	i	Carlisle United
10. Singers FC	j	Coventry City
11. St Domingo FC	k	Leyton Orient
12. New Brompton	l	Newcastle United
13. Glyn Cricket & Football Club	m	Manchester United
14. Ardwick FC	n	Oxford United

15.	Newton Heath	o	Stockport County
16.	Wimbledon	p	Oldham Athletic
17.	Stanley	q	Gillingham
18.	Pine Villa	r	Milton Keynes Dons
19.	Headington	s	Blackpool
20.	St Jude's	t	Tranmere Rovers
21.	Heaton Norris Rovers	u	Bolton
22.	Belmont AFC	v	Cardiff City
23.	Thames Iron Works	w	Bournemouth
24.	St Luke's	x	Manchester City

Answers: 1. (d), 2. (e), 3. (s), 4. (u), 5. (w), 6. (c), 7. (a), 8. (v), 9. (i), 10. (j), 11. (b), 12. (q), 13. (k), 14. (x), 15. (m), 16. (r), 17. (l), 18. (p), 19. (n), 20. (g), 21. (o), 22. (t), 23. (f), 24. (h).

12 TEAMS WHO ARE TOO CLOSE FOR COMFORT

Clubs	**Distance**
1. Dundee & Dundee United	0.22 miles

Dundee/Dundee United

2. Nottingham Forest & Notts County	0.74 miles
3. Liverpool & Everton	0.79 miles
4. Chelsea & Fulham	1.89 miles
5. Aston Villa & Birmingham City	3.50 miles

6.	Hearts & Hibernian	3.55 miles
7.	Sheffield Wednesday & Sheffield United	3.85 miles
8.	West Bromwich Albion & Aston Villa	3.91 miles
9.	Arsenal & Tottenham	3.99 miles
10.	Rangers & Celtic	4.68 miles
11.	Bristol City & Bristol Rovers	4.85 miles
12.	Manchester United & Manchester City	5.17 miles

10 WHO CROSSED A GREAT DIVIDE

1. Mo Johnston

In 1989 Maurice 'Mo' Johnston, was playing with Nantes in France. Glasgow Celtic, Mo's former team and boyhood favourites were in negotiations to bring the player, who had previously scored 55 goals in 99 games for the Bhoys, back to the green and white hoops to revive their flagging fortunes. Johnston had said that he would only go back to Scotland to play for Celtic. He even agreed to appear, at Celtic's urging, at a live press conference announcing to the world that he was going back home to Celtic. The catch was that despite some 'pre-contract agreement' Celtic had not completed the signing; Johnston was still playing for Nantes. The stage was set for Rangers' under-manager Graeme Souness, to step in and offer Mo an unheard-of amount of money to play for Rangers, way beyond what Celtic could deliver. Johnston's name is forever remembered as the first Catholic star to play for Glasgow Rangers, and the first Catholic signing for the club since World War II. Mo's decision infuriated Celtic and Rangers fans alike. Rangers fans were seen on TV burning their season tickets and scarves in bitter protest at the signing of a Catholic and former Celtic player. Celtic fans felt betrayed by their prodigal son and forever henceforth labelled him the greatest soccer Judas in history; when he scored his first goal against Celtic, he received a yellow card for over-celebrating. Since his signing, Catholics have been taken on at an increasing rate at Ibrox and at certain points since then the Rangers squad has included more Catholics than Protestants. While Mo will tell you that he didn't sign to break down any religious barriers, he nonetheless succeeded in doing just that. For this, in some eyes he is more hero than villain.

2. **Sol Campbell**

You can stick your Sol Campbell up your Arse,
You can stick your Sol Campbell up your Arse,
You can stick your Sol Campbell,
Stick your Sol Campbell,
Stick your Sol Campbell up your Arse.

This song conveys the essence of White Hart Lane's response to the former favourite's decision to leave his boyhood club for Arsenal and loads more money. He was considered a 'greedy Judas git' for this, a situation of which he is well aware, as many Spurs fans found the time to mention it to him in another chant. And in February 2006, soon after a half-time exit from Highbury amid reports of 'mental problems', Spurs fans composed this charming verse (to the tune of 'Lord of the Dance'):

Sol, Sol, wherever you may be,
You're on the verge of lunacy ...

and it got much worse.

3. Luís Figo

When Luís Figo returned to the Camp Nou after defecting from Barcelona to Real Madrid for a transfer fee of €37.5 million, he was greeted

Luis Figo: never far from an angry Catalunyan

with a hail of insults, bottles, mobile phones and, remarkably, a pig's head. The Portuguese winger had been braced for a hellish reception from the Barcelona crowd but even he must have been caught off guard by this vast assortment of objects. Lest there was any chance of cooler minds prevailing, Barcelona's president at the time, Joan Gaspart, grunted, 'We're not the villains here. I don't like it when people come to our house and provoke us.'

4. Nick Barmby

Barmby had a bumpy start at Everton following his arrival in '96. He never really showed his true form until the '99/2000 season, when he scored into double figures, was voted the Independent Everton Supporters Player of the Season and was reselected for the England squad, after an absence of three and a half years, for Euro 2000. Barmby returned from that unhappy campaign asking for £25k a week in wages. When Everton reluctantly agreed, Barmby turned it down, saying he wanted £35k. The general conclusion was that he had been headhunted by Chelsea, one of the few teams prepared to pay that sort of money. But then the unpalatable truth became public: Barmby not only wanted to leave Everton, he intended to join arch-rivals Liverpool, the implication being that he had in fact been tapped by all the Reds in the England team at Euro 2000. A £6-million deal was done, and in the blink of an eye Barmby became Public Enemy No 1 for Everton fans, who will never forgive him, though they could at least enjoy a certain amount of Schadenfreude: Barmby's career at Liverpool was hardly stellar, though he did of course fulfil the duty of the ex by scoring against Everton in the derby.

5. **Clyde Wijnhard**

The Dutch striker is widely reviled at Huddersfield Town. After nearly losing an arm in a car accident, Town stood by him throughout his two-year recovery, and then, as soon as he was fit, he was off like a rat up a drainpipe. The following season when Huddersfield played rivals Oldham, Wijnhard single-handedly tore them apart and even bothered to take the piss out of the away fans when he scored, the bad, bad lad.

6. **Ron 'I'll never leave Sheffield Wednesday' Atkinson**

One week later he was Ron 'Manager of Aston Villa' Atkinson.

7. **John Toshack**

Installed as Welsh manager in 2004, Toshack is unpopular

in Cardiff for his decision to become player-coach at Swansea and make them into a good side when he cut his teeth in management in the late '70s and early '80s. He transformed the Jacks, taking them from the old Fourth Division all the way to the top-flight in just four seasons – an achievement for which he was rewarded with an OBE. He achieved this by bringing his old Liverpool mates down to play for the club, when, by rights, he should have gone and done that job for his hometown team, where he began his career. This period of unparalleled Swansea success included an episode in which Toshack kissed his Swansea badge in front of 'the Bob', (the stand for Cardiff City diehards) in sight of the house in which he was born. It really doesn't get any worse than that.

8. **Marc Joseph**

In his Bosman move from Cambridge United to Peterborough in 2001, Joseph illustrates a rivalry that few of us even know exists. The defender – whose inability to score gave him something verging on cult status for the Cambridge – netted on his debut for the Posh. The only small consolation for U's fans in his treacherous move, the 'at least-he'll-never-score-for-them' factor, was wiped out in his first 90 minutes at his new club. On his return to the Abbey for the 'Cambridgeshire Derby' he was mercilessly abused, booed and jeered at at every opportunity until he put the ball into the net for the second time in his career. At this point he gave it to the Newmarket Road End for a good 20 seconds before he realised the offside flag was raised. This flag was, of course, glorious good news to the home crowd, whose chants are totally unprintable.

9. **Alan 'I'll never leave Leeds' Smith**

When he became Alan 'I Play for Man United Now' Smith in 2004, crossing the Pennines in a £7-million deal, the England forward found himself vilified by the Leeds fans for joining the club they hate the most, while his previous badge-kissing devotion to the Whites' cause did nothing to endear him to the Old Trafford faithful either. Feelings in Yorkshire ran so high that he was initially unable to return to Elland Road for Lucas Radebe's testimonial because of concerns over security.

10. **Barry Siddall**

Goalkeeper Siddall left Port Vale for local rivals Stoke City, returned to Vale Park with Blackpool a while later, and, following heckling from the Bycars End, lifted up his 'keeper's shirt to reveal a Stoke top! Appalling behaviour, give the man a medal.

THE ONE PLAYER TO HAVE PLAYED IN THE MANCHESTER, MERSEYSIDE AND GLASGOW DERBIES

Is Andrei Kanchelskis, of:

Dynamo Kiev, Shakhtar Donetsk, **Manchester United**, **Everton**, Fiorentina, **Rangers**, Manchester City, Southampton, Al-Hilal, Dinamo Moscow and FC Saturn Moscow.

Andrei Kanchelskis' name, incidentally, is an anagram of *'He's a lad in knickers'*.

CITY CITY XI

1 Jon Sheffield

2 Clark Carlisle

5 Alan Cork

6 Douglas Freedman

3 Justin Edinburgh

7 Milan Baros

4 Rio Ferdinand

8 Alan Sunderland

10 Sydney Govou

9 Dion Dublin

11 Dwight Yorke

Due to injury and suspension, some out-field players are being played out of position in the Word XIs

MEASURE AND SHAPE

STATTO CORNER

HOW WOMEN'S FOOTBALL BATTLED FOR SURVIVAL

By Patricia Gregory

THE 8 STADIA IN EUROPE WITH 80,000-PLUS CAPACITY
THE 10 BIGGEST STADIA
CHAMPIONS LEAGUE TRIVIA
HIGHEST AVERAGE GATES: EUROPE 2003–2004
WINNERS OF THE BALLON D'OR
FIFA WORLD PLAYER OF THE YEAR (MALE)
FIFA WORLD PLAYER OF THE YEAR (FEMALE)
THE TOP 20 MOST CAPPED PLAYERS
ENGLAND'S TOP GOALSCORERS
THE TRIPLICATED CUP TIE
FA CUP FINALISTS WHO HAVE NEVER WON THE FA CUP
THE GAME OF 3 HALVES

HOW WOMEN'S FOOTBALL BATTLED FOR SURVIVAL

BBC Sport's **Patricia Gregory**, who helped found the women's FA in the 1960s, charts how the game overcame prejudice and scorn in its early days

Department of Culture Media and Sport figures show that Football is the most popular women's sport in England, the number of women and girls participating in football exceeding 100,000 with over 62,000 registered women players. It was not always so.

The earliest recorded women's football match anywhere in the world took place in 1895 in North London. During the First World War the female workers of the munitions factories used to play matches because men were away fighting the war. But in 1921 the FA became concerned that money raised ostensibly for charitable purposes was not finding its way to such organisations. Their response was to pass a rule forbidding women from playing football, and that rule remained in force until December 1969. This did not deter such stalwarts as the Dick Kerr's Ladies of Preston (who, on Boxing Day 1920, played a game at Goodison Park against St Helen's Ladies in front of 53,000 spectators – the largest crowd ever seen at a women's football match in Britain) nor the Manchester Corinthians – but the spur for the growth of the game came with England's 1966 World Cup victory.

Clubs began to appear, although it was difficult at first to locate them, and in 1967 my team (White Ribbon – we used the training facilities of an amateur men's side called 'White Star' in Tottenham) was contacted by Arthur Hobbs, who was organising the Deal tournament for Ladies' Football (as it was then known). Arthur knew that we needed to be organised and over the next few years we formed our teams into leagues, and in late 1969 the Ladies' FA of Great Britain was born. The name was swiftly changed to the Women's FA as we were advised that 'women's' was a more inclusive word than 'ladies' – judged more suitable for the demurer pastime of golf!

In those days we included in our number the few teams of Northern Ireland, Scotland and Wales, but eventually the other British men's associations pointed out that we could not govern their teams. Initially the FA was reluctant to alter its rules but constant representation brought about the rescinding of the 1921 rule so that our teams could play on local park pitches and use official referees, as they were no longer considered to be unaffiliated.

In late 1971, UEFA was becoming concerned that here was a branch of football which needed to be controlled, and in a historic vote, 31 countries voted in favour with one against (Scotland) to bring women's football into the fold. In February 1972, the FA chose to recognise the WFA as 'the sole governing body of women's football in this country at the present time'. It didn't give us much but it was a step forward.

For the next 20 years the WFA struggled against the odds to establish women's football:

- The WFA Cup began in 1971 with sponsorship from Mitre;

- There was financial and other support from the Sports Council and the Central Council of Physical Recreation;

- The WFA registered women referees until the Sex Discrimination Act came into force and the FA had to concede that women could be registered with their County Association;

- The first official England team was formed and their first opponents were Scotland in Greenock on 18 November 1972 – coincidentally exactly 100 years after the first men's international which was played in Glasgow. The result? A 3–2 victory over Scotland.

In the mid-'80s the WFA was granted affiliation to the FA and a seat on the Council, but the struggle was hard and in 1993 it was somewhat reluctantly decided to hand over the day-to-day running of the game to the FA. The progress has been enormous, with the clubs/leagues still run by those thousands of anonymous people who give their time and effort selflessly – just like the boys'/men's clubs up and down the country. Today, football has replaced netball as the most popular sport among girls in the UK. How far we have come.

THE 8
STADIA IN EUROPE WITH 80,000-PLUS CAPACITY

Opened in 1957 with an inauguration service including a solemn mass and a blessing of the stadium by the Archbishop of Barcelona

	Stadium	Capacity	City
1.	L'Estadi (Camp Nou)	98,800	Barcelona
2.	Stadio Giuseppe Meazza (San Siro)	85,700	AC Milan
3.	Olimpiyskiy Stadion	83,160	Kiyiv (Kiev)
4.	Croke Park	82,500	Dublin (Gaelic Football)
5.	Stadio Olimpico	82,300	AS Roma
6.	Atatürk Olympic Stadium	82,000	Istanbul
7.	Luzniki	80,480	Moscow
8.	Stade de France	80,000	Saint-Denis

THE 10 BIGGEST STADIA

	Country	Use	Name	Capacity
1.	USA	Race-use	Indianapolis Motor Speedway	250,000
2.	JPN	Horse-Racing	Tokyo Racecourse, Tokyo	223,000
3.	CZE	Multi-use	Praha Velk˘ Strahovsk˘ Stadion	220,000
4.	CHN	Race-use	Shanghai Int'l Circuit, Shanghai	200,000
5.	USA	Race-use	Daytona Int'l Speedway, Daytona Beach	168,000
6.	USA	Race-use	Lowe's Motor Speedway, Concord	167,000
7.	JPN	Horse-Racing	Nakayama Racecourse, Chiba	165,676
8.	USA	Race-use	Bristol Motor Speedway, Bristol	160,000
9.	USA	Race-use	Texas Motor Speedway, Justin	154,861
Joint 10.	PRK	Multi-use	May Day Stadium Pyöngyang Rungnado	150,000
Joint 10.	DEU	Race-use	Nürburgring Nürburg	150,000

It may be a surprise to find that no purpose-built football ground makes the top ten. The highest capacity football stadium in the world is the *Jornalista Mário Filho* in Rio de Janeiro. Better known as the Maracaña, the stadium can hold 103,045 spectators, of which 77,743 can be seated. In the 1950 World Cup final between Uruguay and Brazil, it was estimated that 200,000 fans were in the stadium, many people finding an illegal way to enter. This figure represents the largest crowd ever to attend a football match.

CHAMPIONS LEAGUE TRIVIA

1. In the 2005 final all 11 goals, including the 5 of the penalty shoot-out, were scored at the same end.

2. Bob Paisley is the only man to coach 3 Champions Cup-winning sides, with Liverpool FC in 1977, 1978 and 1981.

3. Milan is the only city that has won the Champions Cup with two different teams: Inter & Milan (the two clubs have won 8 cups in total).

4. Real Madrid have the record number of consecutive participations in the Champions Cup with 15 from 1955/56 to 1969/70.

5. Five clubs have been awarded the trophy permanently:
   - Real Madrid, who won the first five competitions from 1956 to 1960.
   - Ajax, who won consecutively in 1971–73.
   - Bayern Munich, winner of the next three competitions in 1974–76.
   - Milan, who won for the fifth time in 1994.
   - Liverpool, whose 2005 win was also their fifth.

6. Real Madrid CF has won this competition 9 times. The next most successful teams are AC Milan (6 titles), Liverpool FC (5 titles), Bayern Munich and AFC Ajax (4 titles).

7. Clarence Seedorf is the only player to win the Cup with 3 different teams:

Ajax Amsterdam	1995
Real Madrid	1998
AC Milan	2003

8. Paolo Maldini of Milan scored the fastest ever goal in Champions League in the 2005 final against Liverpool: 53 seconds. At 37 years of age he was also the oldest scorer in Champions League final.

9. Nottingham Forest are the only club to have won the European Cup more times (twice) than they have won their domestic league (once). Forest won the English League in 1978 before winning the European Cup in 1979 and defending it in 1980.

10. Five players have scored a hat-trick on their debut in the Champions League:

Marco van Basten (AC Milan)	1992
Faustino Asprilla (Newcastle United)	1997
Yakubu Aiyegbeni (Maccabi Haifa)	2002
Wayne Rooney (Manchester United)	2004
Vincenzo Iaquinta (Udinese)	2005

11. In September 2005 Raúl became the first player in the history of the competiton to reach 50 goals by scoring in Real Madrid's 2–1 victory over Olympiakos.

12. In the 50 years since the competition began in 1955 only 4 derbies have been played:

Real Madrid 2–1 Atlético de Madrid	1958/59	Semi-final
Internazionale 1–1 AC Milan	2002/03	Semi-final *
Chelsea 3–2 Arsenal	2003/04	Quarter-final
Internazionale 0–3 (ab) AC Milan	2004/05	Quarter-final †

*Though the teams share the same stadium, AC Milan went through on away goals, Andriy Shevchenko scoring the vital 'away' goal on his own ground.

† The second leg was abandoned because of disturbances among the Inter fans. Inter were 3–0 down on aggregate at the time. The tie was awarded to AC.

HIGHEST AVERAGE GATES: EUROPE 2003–2004

1. **Germany**   37,500

Kaiserslautern: the best fans in the Bundesliga, according to them

2.	**England**	35,000
3.	**Spain**	28,800
4.	**Italy**	25,500
5.	**France**	20,100
6.	**Turkey**	16,800
7.	**Netherlands**	16,000
8.	**Scotland**	15,200
9.	**Russia**	11,600
10.	**Belgium**	9900
11.	**Sweden**	9800
12.	**Portugal**	9500
13.	**Switzerland**	9000

14.	**Denmark**	8000
15.	**Norway**	8000
16.	**Austria**	7200
17.	**Romania**	7200
18.	**Greece**	5800
19.	**Poland**	5500
20.	**Czech Republic**	4800
21.	**Hungary**	3300
22.	**Croatia**	2600
23.	**Finland**	2600
24.	**Ireland**	1800
25.	**Wales**	300

WINNERS OF THE BALLON D'OR

The Golden Ball – known in English as the European Footballer of the Year Award – was created in 1956 by the French football magazine *France Football*.

2005	**Ronaldinho**	FC Barcelona
2004	**Andriy Shevchenko**	AC Milan
2003	**Pavel Nedved**	Juventus
2002	**Ronaldo**	Real Madrid
2001	**Michael Owen**	Liverpool
2000	**Luis Figo**	Real Madrid
1999	**Rivaldo**	FC Barcelona
1998	**Zinedine Zidane**	Juventus
1997	**Ronaldo**	Inter Milan
1996	**Matthias Sammer**	Borussia Dortmund

1995	**George Weah**	AC Milan
1994	**Hristo Stoitchkov**	FC Barcelona
1993	**Roberto Baggio**	Juventus
1992	**Marco van Basten**	AC Milan
1991	**Jean-Pierre Papin**	Olympique Marseille
1990	**Lothar Matthäus**	Inter Milan
1989	**Marco van Basten**	AC Milan
1988	**Marco van Basten**	AC Milan
1987	**Ruud Gullit**	AC Milan
1986	**Igor Belanov**	Dynamo Kiev
1985	**Michel Platini**	Juventus
1984	**Michel Platini**	Juventus
1983	**Michel Platini**	Juventus
1982	**Paolo Rossi**	Juventus
1981	**Karl-Heinz Rummenigge**	Bayern Munich
1980	**Karl-Heinz Rummenigge**	Bayern Munich
1979	**Kevin Keegan**	Hamburger SV
1978	**Kevin Keegan**	Hamburger SV
1977	**Allan Simonsen**	Borussia Monchengladbach
1976	**Franz Beckenbauer**	Bayern Munich
1975	**Oleg Blokhin**	Dynamo Kiev
1974	**Johan Cruyff**	Ajax Amsterdam
1973	**Johan Cruyff**	Ajax Amsterdam
1972	**Franz Beckenbauer**	Bayern Munich
1971	**Johan Cruyff**	Ajax Amsterdam
1970	**Gerd Müller**	Bayern Munich
1969	**Gianni Rivera**	AC Milan
1968	**George Best**	Manchester United
1967	**Flórián Albert**	Ferencvaros

1966	**Bobby Charlton**	Manchester United
1965	**Eusebio**	Benfica
1964	**Denis Law**	Manchester United
1963	**Lev Yashin**	Dynamo Moscow
1962	**Josef Masopust**	Dukla Prague
1961	**Omar Sivori**	Juventus
1960	**Luis Suárez**	FC Barcelona
1959	**Alfredo Di Stefano**	Real Madrid
1958	**Raymond Kopa**	Real Madrid
1957	**Alfredo Di Stefano**	Real Madrid
1956	**Stanley Matthews**	Blackpool

Players turning out for Italian clubs have the highest strike-rate, winning 17 of the 49 nominations. The Dutch and Germans tie for most players by nation with seven wins each. Lev Yashin is the only goalkeeper to take the prize; when asked for his secret, he would say the trick was to 'have a smoke to calm your nerves, then toss back a strong drink to tone your muscles'.

FIFA WORLD PLAYER OF THE YEAR (MALE)

An award started in 1991, given annually to the male and (since 2001) female player who is thought to be the best in the world, based on votes by coaches and captains of international teams.

2005	**Ronaldinho**	Brazil
2004	**Ronaldinho**	Brazil
2003	**Zinedine Zidane**	France

2002	**Ronaldo**	Brazil
2001	**Luis Figo**	Portugal
2000	**Zinedine Zidane**	France
1999	**Rivaldo**	Brazil
1998	**Zinedine Zidane**	France
1997	**Ronaldo**	Brazil
1996	**Ronaldo**	Brazil
1995	**George Weah**	Liberia
1994	**Romario**	Brazil
1993	**Roberto Baggio**	Italy
1992	**Marco van Basten**	Holland
1991	**Lothar Matthäus**	Germany

FIFA WORLD PLAYER OF THE YEAR (FEMALE)

Triple World Player of the Year, Birgit Prinz

2005	**Birgit Prinz**	Germany
2004	**Birgit Prinz**	Germany
2003	**Birgit Prinz**	Germany
2002	**Mia Hamm**	United States
2001	**Mia Hamm**	United States

THE TOP 20 MOST CAPPED PLAYERS

1. **Mohamed Al-Deayea**
   Saudi Arabia   173   (1990–2004) ★
2. **Claudio Suárez**
   Mexico   172   (1992–2004) ★
3. **Cobi Jones**
   USA   164   (1992–2004) ★
   Adnan Kh. Al-Talyani
   UAE   164   (1984–1997)
5. **Hossam Hassan**
   Egypt   163   (1985–2004) ★
6. **Sami Al-Jaber**
   Saudi Arabia   152   (1992–2005) ★
7. **Lothar Matthäus**
   (West) Germany   150   (1980–2000)
8. **Mohammed Al-Khilaiwi**
   Saudi Arabia   143   (1990–2001)
   Marko Kristal
   Estonia   143   (1992–2005) ★
   Thomas Ravelli
   Sweden   143   (1981–1997)
   Martin Reim
   Estonia   143   (1992–2005) ★
12. **Ali Daei**
    Iran   142   (1993–2005) ★
13. **Majed Abdullah**
    Saudi Arabia   139   (1978–1994)
14. **Cafu**
    Brazil   135   (1990–2005) ★
    Myung-Bo Hong
    South Korea   135   (1990–2002)
16. **Jeff Agoos**
    USA   134   (1988–2003) ★

17. **Bashar Abdullah**
    Kuwait   131   (1996–2005) *

18. **Jorge Campos**
    Mexico   130   (1991–2003) *

19. **Peter Schmeichel**
    Denmark   129   (1987–2001) *

20. **Marcelo Balboa**
    USA   128   (1988–2000) *

* Denotes players still active as of January 2006.

ENGLAND'S TOP GOALSCORERS

Player	Clubs/Career	Gls	Gms
Bobby Charlton	(Manchester United, 1958–70)	49	106
Gary Lineker	(Leicester, Everton, Barcelona, Spurs, 1984–92)	48	80
Jimmy Greaves	(Chelsea, Tottenham Hotspur, 1959–67)	44	57
Michael Owen	(Liverpool, R/Madrid, Newcastle, 1998–present)	33	74*
Nat Lofthouse	(Bolton Wanderers, 1951–59)	30	33
Alan Shearer	(Southampton, Blackburn, Newcastle, 1992–2000)	30	63
Tom Finney	(Preston North End, 1947–59)	30	76
VJ Woodward	(Tottenham Hotspur, Chelsea, 1903–11)	29	23
Steve Bloomer	(Derby County, Middlesbrough, 1895–1907)	28	23
David Platt	(Villa, Bari, Juve, Sampdoria, Arsenal, 1990–96)	27	62

* Still active. Figure as of January 2006.

THE TRIPLICATED CUP TIE

Some teams seem to have a magnetic attraction to each other when the balls come out of the hat for Cup ties, but the odds of the following happening are roughly two million to one:

1955–56 in the 3rd round of the FA Cup. Leeds United vs Cardiff City

1956–57 in the 3rd round of the FA Cup, Leeds United vs Cardiff City

1957–58 in the 3rd round of the FA Cup, Leeds United vs Cardiff City

Outcomes:

1955–56: Cardiff beat Leeds 2–1 after a goalless first half.

1956–57: Cardiff beat Leeds 2–1 after a goalless first half.

1957–58: Cardiff beat Leeds 2–1 …

Although the first half wasn't goalless, with a minute to go the score was 2–1 to Cardiff. Wilbur Cash was brought down and Leeds appealed for a penalty. Not given, and Cardiff win by the same score in the same fixture for the third season running.

FA CUP FINALISTS WHO HAVE NEVER WON THE FA CUP

Club	Number of Finals
Leicester City	4
Birmingham City	2
Queen's Park (Glasgow)	2
Bristol City	1
Luton Town	1
Fulham	1
Queens Park Rangers	1
Brighton and Hove Albion	1
Watford	1
Crystal Palace	1
Middlesbrough	1
Millwall	1

THE GAME OF 3 HALVES

On the first day of the 1894–95 season Sunderland were at home to Derby County. The official referee was late, and the game started with a deputy in charge. The two teams played for 45 minutes and then the official referee arrived. What should he do?

Obvious:

The official referee decided to give Derby, who were losing 3–0, the option of starting the game again. Surprisingly, or perhaps not, they took it, and it became known as 'the game of three halves'.

Derby lost the toss twice and were forced to kick against a strong gale for the first two halves. The press had already reported that Sunderland were leading 3–0 at half-time, a scoreline that Derby helped them to repeat.

The game eventually finished 8–0, Sunderland actually winning 11–0 over the three halves.

LIVING THINGS

SICK AS THE PARROT WHO ATE ALL THE PIES

MEMORIES OF THE BARCLAY
By **Edward Banks**

10 ALMOST-FORGOTTEN HALF-TIME SNACKS
LARD XI
FOODIE XI
11 ANIMALS ON THE PITCH
NOAH'S XI
10 STREAKERS
4 FOOTBALLERS' WIVES AND 2 CONSORTS

MEMORIES OF THE BARCLAY

Canaries follower **Edward Banks** on the matter of refreshments

Today, amongst other comestible items, it is possible to find a 'guest' pie flavoured with lamb, chick peas and mint on the menu at our home ground at Carrow Road. While the prices are not what they used to be, there can be few followers of our national game who would not applaud such a development. Many visiting supporters comment on it, because who amongst us has not had occasion to lament the quality of food available to the hungry fan? Though one sometimes encounters the unexpected delight – the butter pies at Preston North End spring to mind – sadly these moments to savour tend to be the exception rather than the rule.

You need not cast the mind back too far to recollect an era when all the working man had to satisfy him was a beef rissole on a bap – which in those days went by the name 'hamburger' rather than the more fashionable beefburger of latter years, albeit, in truth, the one was hardly distinguishable from the other. It was either that, or a hot dog of dubious origin.

It has to be said, though, that however disappointing the article itself might turn out to be, the aroma of frying onions drew one along the banks of the River Wensum towards the thrill of the game, our own 'little scrimmage' as we put it in our famous song 'On the Ball City' (the oldest of all football chants to remain in popular use, incidentally, dating back to 1905). All this formed an integral backdrop to the Saturday afternoon, a part that one would not like to see vanish entirely, even with the advent of improved catering. Not all change is for the good – it is to be hoped that the half-time beef tea can survive, that it won't become subject to a health and safety banning order for being 'dangerously hot' in these days of the 'energy drink'.

Our new menu provokes in me a distinct memory of an episode concerning my father's old terrace companion, my Uncle Jack. Uncle Jack was a 'character' – he was once turned away from the turnstile for concealing in his overcoat a ferret that he had picked up at the Cattle Market earlier in the day. The episode in question concerns the time when he mounted a campaign to have his favourite 'Calcy's Caramac' chocolate bar stocked by the in-ground catering concession. His view was that not only was the Caramac a superior confection to the ubiquitous Wagon Wheel, but that also, being produced in the city, it would benefit the local economy. It seemed, though, that Burton's – the manufacturers of the Wagon Wheel – had secured the monopoly at football clubs across the land, and despite a letter to City Hall the matter was never taken seriously. The council merely stated that he was well within his rights to take his own choice of snack along to the ground should he so wish. This rather overlooked his main argument, viz., that it was difficult to prevent the chocolate melting in his pocket in the crush of the old standing terrace at the Barclay End, a matter which, as he was at pains to point out, could easily have been remedied were it only possible to purchase it direct from the hut at half-time. My father still mentions it to this day.

On the Ball, City!

10
ALMOST-FORGOTTEN HALF-TIME SNACKS

Not a Caley's Caramac

1. WAGON WHEELS

The chocolate-coated, marshmallow biscuit can still be found at certain grounds, much to the chagrin of Edward Banks' Uncle Jack, but have you ever seen anybody actually buy one?

2. **Clix**

A chewing gum that you pushed out of a foil-backed plastic wrapper and left stuck to the underside of the crush barrier at the final whistle.

3. **Fish 'n' Chips**

Not real fish and chips, the fish 'n' chip-shaped, biscuit-like, flavoured item that tasted of neither fish nor chips.

4. **Smiths Maxi Sacks**

Huge bags of crisps that could last until full time. Very popular at Port Vale.

5. **Fruit Salads**

Thrown from a mascot Moose's bucket at Cambridge United, in exchange for loose change (and washers, rusty nails etc) for charity.

6. **Uncle Joe's Mint Balls**

There are still old blokes who can be found dealing these on the terraces. Accept the offer only if you want everything you eat and drink for the next three days to provoke a vile cough-mixture-like aftertaste.

7. **Chomp Bars**

At away games Brentford supporters apparently hurl these chewy little caramel bars onto the pitch in great numbers to the tribal chants of 'Chomp! Chomp! Chomp!'

8. **Strawberry liquorice shoelaces**

Popular at Grimsby, apparently; good for hanging yourself with.

9. Cough Candy

A chap could be seen walking around the Bloomfield Rd Kop, Blackpool, *c.*1967, selling quarter bags of this excellent emollient sweet.

10. Polos

The circular mint with the hole in the middle, to remind you of how many you've scored.

LARD XI

1. William 'Fatty' Foulke

Don't call him late for dinner

'You can call me anything but don't call me late for dinner', was the catchphrase of Sheffield United's famous goalkeeper and captain at the turn of the twentieth century. Clocking in at somewhere between 22 and 26 stone (reports vary), he eclipsed much of the target area with sheer bulk and reputedly had his teammates tie his bootlaces for him. Foulke left the Blades for Chelsea in 1905, for a transfer fee of £50. He took his new London teammates by surprise by entering the canteen before the rest of them and eating all eleven breakfasts.

2. Jan Molby

Built like a beer keg, Jan spent a short time in a fat farm at Her Majesty's Pleasure in the 1988/89 season when he was jailed for three months for reckless driving after turning his BMW over outside a nightclub. Many fans remarked that the Great Dane (nickname: *Carlsberg*) returned to the side looking fitter and trimmer than he had for years after his sentence had been completed.

3. **Thomas Brolin**

Something of a legend for the Swedish National side – finding the net a total of 26 times in 47 appearances – the podgy cherub managed just four goals in his disappointing season at Leeds United, the beginning of a decline that saw him give up the game in 1998, citing a lack of motivation. A player who always pissed the fatness test, his most memorable moment for Leeds came against Sheffield Wednesday when the ball hit his ample backside and ended up in the net. When he later signed for Crystal Palace, TV pundit Frank McClintock was heard to muse, 'What is Brolin's role? Catering manager?' After leaving football, Thomas returned to Sweden and involved himself in any number of business ventures before establishing the restaurant *Undici* in Stockholm. Undici – meaning 11 in Italian, after the number he wore for Parma – is a buzzing eaterie that combines the cuisine of Brolin's native northern Sweden with that of his adopted home of Italy. Thommo also starred in a jacuzzi advert, and hit the headlines after his car collided with an elk.

4. **Kevin Davies**

When Kevin was on loan at Millwall, Steve Claridge reckoned that he came out of the shower with the towel up under his armpits to cover his 'man boobs'.

5. **Paul Gascoigne**

In his early days Gazza was a bonny little scamp. In case he should ever forget this fact, supporters of opposing sides routinely pelted him with Mars Bars. While England manager Graham Taylor referred obliquely to his 'refuelling issues', Dino Zoff who managed him at Lazio was more specific. 'He ate ice cream for breakfast, he drank beer for lunch, and when he was injured he blew up like a whale,' Zoff said, before adding the qualifying: 'But as a player? Oh, beautiful, beautiful.'

6. **Neville Southall**

Forever taking goal kicks in front of opposing fans to the sound of *Oooohhaaargggyorsshityoufatbastard*, by the end of his career the Everton keeper was reputedly having his shorts specially adapted to get round the circumference of his southern hemisphere.

7. **Maradona**

In 2000, FIFA chose Pele and Maradona as the sport's greatest players: Pele topped a 'football family' poll – consisting of FIFA officials, national team coaches and journalists – while Maradona was favoured by fans who cast their votes on FIFA's official website. Eric Cantona once remarked that, 'In the course of time it will be said that Maradona was to football what Rimbaud was to poetry and Mozart to music.' During his 20–year career, Maradona led Argentina to the World Cup title in 1986, and the final in 1990. The genius from Buenos Aires – who has a travelling museum in his honour in that city – was distinguished by a low centre of gravity and, even at his peak, a tendency to carry extra weight. Since quitting professional soccer in 1997, Maradona grew unrecognisably fat as he struggled to overcome cocaine addiction. He has repeatedly been hospitalised because of severe health problems brought on by drug abuse and overeating, and has undergone surgery to limit the stomach's capacity for holding food by bypassing part of the small intestine. Much as the English revile Maradona – as a consequence of the Hand of God – it's hard to poke fun at a player of his genius. Hard, but not impossible.

8. Mickey Quinn

Self-styled cult legend, Quinn's autobiography is titled *Who Ate All the Pies?* He scored 230 goals in 512 league games for six football clubs, including Newcastle United, Coventry City and Portsmouth and became infamous for his love of women, gambling, drinking and fighting – with Peter Schmeichel on the pitch, and John Fashanu off it. Here is a sample from an online Q&A with Mickey Quinn, reprinted with thanks to *Guardian Online*:

Q. Cheese or chocolate?

A. You know, I'm partial to a bit of the old cheddar to tell you the truth.

Q. That's not all you're partial to, is it ... Sumo? Is it really true that you ate all the pies?

A. *(Laughs)* Well I didn't eat them all, but it's probably fair to say that I ate more than my fair share.

Q. So as a connoisseur, what's your favourite filling?

A. Oh it's got to be chicken and mushroom, without a doubt.

9. **Ronaldo**

Persistent rumours abound about the weight of the European Player of the Year, 1997 and 2002.

When asked about this, following his hat-trick against Argentina in a World Cup qualifier in 2004, Brazil manager Mario Zagallo retorted, 'They say Ronaldo is fat. Well, I for one would love to have eleven 'fat' players like Ronaldo in my side.'

Good point, Mario.

Javier Zanetti, who played with the Brazilian at Inter Milan, said, 'The only way to stop Ronaldo is to catch him when he starts his runs, and then shout for help from some team mates.' Of his unusual penalty hat-trick against Argentina in a World Cup qualifier in June 2004, Zanetti went on to say: 'During the game he was giving instructions to his defence to try and sort things out. Some people say he's fat, but as far as I can remember he was even heavier when he was in Italy. As a human being though, he is superb, very grounded.'

10. **Bjarni Gudjonsson**

Icelandic winger, often pilloried during his time at Stoke City for being 'a titchy little fat bastard.' The nincompoops who shouted this at him failed to note he was Stoke's best (Icelandic) player.

11. **Mark McGhee**

He's fat,
He's round,
He's worth a million pounds,
Mark McGhee, Mark McGhee.

As the star of Celtic's centenary season (1987/88)

the Jungle faithful at Parkhead paid due homage to McGhee's every netbuster with this terrace classic. You have to fear for the future of this song as training regimes and fad diets tend evermore to the elimination of porkers from our game.

FOODIE XI

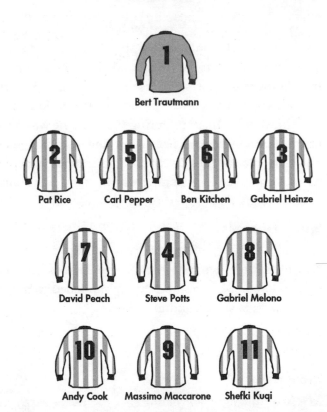

Bert Trautmann

Pat Rice   Carl Pepper   Ben Kitchen   Gabriel Heinze

David Peach   Steve Potts   Gabriel Melono

Andy Cook   Massimo Maccarone   Shefki Kuqi

11 ANIMALS ON THE PITCH

1. The fox in the box

In November 1996 the Parkhead pitch was encroached upon by a fox. Referee Hugh Dallas was forced to delay a Celtic corner as the intruder gave several players the slip before dashing back into the crowd. Celtic public relations manager Peter McLean said, 'We were very impressed with the pace of the fox. It still hasn't been caught. We don't know how it got in or how it escaped. We have even been given the brush-off by its agent.'

2. The black cat

In April 2005 a black cat ran on to the Deepdale pitch and down the touchline during Preston's 3–0 win over Brighton. As it scampered towards its subsequent escape, fans substituted 'cat' for 'attack' as they chanted: A cat, a cat; a cat, a cat, a cat!

It brought them enough luck to make it to the Championship play-off final (where the good fortune finally ran out as West Ham beat the Lilywhites 1–0).

3. A squirrel

Enlivened matters by bouncing over the pitch in Stevenage's FA Cup fourth qualifying round tie with Bath City in 1999. Someone said it must be nuts to want to watch the rubbish on offer.

4. The duck

In 1976, during a Bundesliga match between Bayern Munich and VfL Bochum, a duck landed close to legendary German goalkeeper Sepp Maier's six-yard box and started prancing about. Maier approached stealthily and leapt at it, arms outstretched. He missed it completely, scoring a duck at duck-catching.

5. **The duck II (the nightmare continues)**

Finnish Division One side TPS took on KuPS in 2005, when suddenly a duck joined the proceedings. The hapless creature was in the wrong place at the wrong time as KuPS' Seth Ablade took a corner that hit the duck and knocked it unconscious (if only he'd been at a funfair – he'd have won a goldfish). Thanks to the presence of a few versatile firemen the duck's life was saved and it was able to fly off safe and sound.

6. **Three pigs vs the wolf**

When Wolverhampton Wanderers visited Bristol City in November '98, Wolfie, the Wolves mascot, was seen goading the Bristol mascots, who were (of course) three little piggies dressed in dungarees. One of the pigs took umbrage and threw a punch which connected with the big bad one. The wolf retaliated with a left hook, whereupon a full-scale brawl broke out, to the great joy of the crowd. Afterwards the policeman in charge of security said no arrests had been made, characterising the incident as, 'Just a lot of huffing and puffing, really.'

7. **The rabbit**

At the Bernabeu in 1997 during a Spanish League game between Real Madrid and Betis, a rabbit jumped (or was thrown, more likely) onto the pitch. There was a pause in the game as Real's Carlos Secretario caught it in a lightning-fast move. Commentator Arsénio Iglesias said: 'Secretario may or may not be a good player, but he is indeed a great hunter.'

8. Billy the Fish

In January 2005 the river Petteril broke its banks and, in the worst floods to hit the city since 1822, poured 20 million litres of water onto the pitch at Brunton Park, home of Carlisle United. During the clear-up operation, the chairman's daughter found a goldfish flapping around in the goalmouth at the waterworks end. The hapless Eurasian carp had been washed out of a tank in a nearby flooded house, but the rescue was a complete success and 'Billy' lived happily ever after in a new bowl.

9. The animal lover

A stray dog came onto the field during the quarter final of the 1962 World Cup game between England and Brazil in Chile: Jimmy Greaves chased it around the pitch and eventually caught it by getting down on all fours and barking – in the excitement the dog pissed all over Greavsie's shirt. Brazilian playmaker Manoel Francisco dos Santos, better known as Garrincha – *Little Bird* – was in hysterics over the incident and adopted the animal. Garrincha was a well-known animal lover of whom it is reported in all seriousness (in Ruy Castro's book, *Garrincha*) that he lost his virginity to a goat.

10. Danger mouse

Early on in an FA Cup third round replay in January 2006 at The Lamb – home of Conference side Tamworth – a mouse scuttled onto the pitch directly in front of the visiting Stoke City fans. It parked up in the right back position of the penalty box (falling into the offside trap).

Every time play came into the area the Stoke supporters could be heard to squeal, 'Ooh aagh, ohh noo, argh', as the mouse came within whiskers of copping it under a set of studs. In their alarm, the crowd urgently started to sing, 'Save the Mouse, Save the Mouse, Save the Mouse.' When no action was taken, they began chanting, 'Simo, Simo, Save the Mouse' to bemused 'keeper Steve Simonsen. After about 15 minutes of intense peril, a Tamworth player eventually spotted the creature and picked it up. It appeared the mouse must have bitten him, because he threw it to a steward as if it were a live device.

11. **Sign him up**

The Knave of Clubs were playing Newcastle Town in the Staffordshire Sunday Cup and were losing 2–0.

A Knave's player was running down the field with only the goalkeeper to beat. He tried a shot from 15 yards out and miscued it, so it was going well wide. A mongrel dog ran onto the field, jumped up at the ball and headed it – the ball flew into the net. The decision given was a goal for Knave of Clubs, though Newcastle Town did hold on to win 3–2.

NOAH'S XI

Peter 'The Cat' Bonetti

Andy Griffin   Steed Malbranque   Glenn Cockerill   Ritchie Partridge

Ruel Fox   Gary Teale   Louis Boa Morte

Steve Bull   Shaun Goater   Gavin Peacock

10 STREAKERS

1. The French incorrect

At the Euro 2000 final a French female covered in white body-dust made out like a member of the Ballet Rambert. She also kept her white translucent leggings on. Tres chic, if not exactly a streak.

2. The Italian incorrect

The French female was joined by an Italian female (the match, between France and Italy, was won by France, 2–1, thanks to David Trezeguet's golden goal). The Italian, possibly inspired by renaissance artists, was covered in blue body paint in the design of the Italian strip with an immaculate crest on her left breast. She performed some 'Kate Bush' dancing with a flowing ribbon. Also très chic, if not exactly what we're looking for.

3. The front page

Two raunchy stunnas, Vanessa Richards, 23, and Rachel Sadler, 18, got their kits off to cheer up their favourite player Paul Gascoigne. Friends Vanessa and Rachel wanted to put a smile back on Gazza's face after his divorce and drink problems. The pair decided that the best plan would be for Vanessa to don a saucy Father Christmas outfit, while Rachel risked goose pimples in a tinsel thong. They raised a festive cheer as they chased Gazza around the pitch at the Riverside Stadium in Middlesbrough in December 1997 in front of a capacity 35,880 crowd. That's more like it. Gazza must've thought Christmas had come early.

4. The communal

Proving they were not shy, a number of Croatia Zagreb fans indulged in some sort of ritual terrace naturalism during the 1998/99 Champions League Qualifier against Celtic.

5. The professional tool

Mark Roberts has streaked at hundreds of sports events, his first at a football match being during a Merseyside derby at Anfield in 1994. With UK fines totalling more than £1,200, Roberts achieved his lifetime ambition of dangling his wang about in the USA by streaking at the XXXVIII Superbowl in Houston in February 2004. He was fined $1000 by a Texas jury, though prosecutors were pushing for the 39-year-old to be jailed for the greater offence of trespass.

6. **The great British eccentric**

At the *5th British Grand National Mascot Race* – a handicap hurdle for people dressed in animal costumes – held at Huntingdon racecourse in 2003 – Chaddy the Owl (Oldham Athletic's owl-like mascot) stormed to victory. But further back in the field there was chaos as some of the competitors pulled up to take a closer look at a naked female who had cavorted across the track.

7. **The charity**

Aberdeen fan Tony Cowe did his best to raise the spirits of the travelling support during the 2000 Scottish Cup final between Rangers and Aberdeen. His sexy romp across the park, clad only in socks and trainers, was the highlight of the day for the Dons as they lost 4–0 at Hampden Park. As well as raising £600 for the Royal Aberdeen Children's Hospital, his bare-faced cheek had a political angle too – the words 'Keep Clause 28' were daubed on his back.

8. **The little earner**

Plucky mum Michelle Newton revealed why she stripped in front of 48,000 fans: it was for a £50 bet. Michelle, 34, established a place in history in January 2001 – as the first streaker at Sunderland's Stadium of

Light (a ground that suggests a much-too-easy rhyme name change. They really should have thought of that, especially in view of the football that goes on there).

9. **The 'I didn't bring them up to do this'**

Fitness instructor and Crystal Palace fan Kelly Parkes, 21, and her sister Ella, 18, had heads turning when they jointly streaked at a Crystal Palace match for a £10 bet. While the girls made their dash in their birthday suits in October 2000, their dad was easy to identify too: he was the only fan in the stands who was covering his eyes.

10. **The Easter Bunny**

Rather apt for the time of year, in March 2002 the only British football team that is in the Bible* – Queen of the South – saw the vision of a red-haired beauty float across Palmerston Park during a league match against Berwick Rangers. After beating four players and slicing through the midfield with some fantastic twists and turns, 22 year-old Hilary Kerr, the lady in question, was finally brought down by an uncompromising steward at the corner flag.

* *'The queen of the south shall rise up in the judgment with this generation, and shall condemn it; for she came from the uttermost parts of the earth to hear the wisdom of Solomon; and, behold, a greater than Solomon is here.' Matthew 12:42*

4 FOOTBALLERS' WIVES
AND 2 CONSORTS

As with the First Lady of the USA, there is often more interest in the holder of this position than in the subject to whom she is referred.

1. **Karren Brady**

   Known as the 'First Lady of Football', Karren Brady was a director at David Sullivan's Sports Newspapers at 22 years of age, and at 23 became the first (and remains the only) female MD of a professional League club. In her own words, she has transformed Birmingham City from 'a bum club with a bum team' to a Premiership business without a single penny of debt. When the club floated on the AIM in 1997, Karren became the youngest MD of any UK PLC. She has twice sold her husband, Canadian striker and professional nomad (Toronto Blizzards, Birmingham, Stoke, Birmingham, West Brom, Fulham, QPR, Sheffield Utd, Norwich, Sheffield Utd, Derby), Paul Peschisolido. On record as saying, 'The thing with footballers is, in the end, they let you down', her marriage to Peschisolido is impressively long-standing, which is good going when you take into account that 'Pesch' has never rid himself of the fluffy '70s side-parted hair that would have been hopelessly out of date even when it was in vogue. Love is a funny old thing.

2. **Milene Domingues**

   Brazilian ex-wife of Ronaldo – she was dubbed 'Ronaldinha' by the Spanish press – Milene Domingues signed for Atlético Madrid in 2002 for a Spanish record fee of €300,000, from Italian women's Serie A side

Fiamma Monza. From a strictly footballing point of view, the single most impressive fact about Milene is that she is the female world record holder for keepie-uppie: in 55,188 touches, she kept the ball in the air for 9 hrs 6 mins.

3. **Victoria Beckham**

On hearing that Tamzin Outhwaite (a soap actress) wouldn't mind a night with her husband, Victoria responded with the following: *Firstly, Tamzin who, secondly, I think it's disrespectful, and thirdly, as if, love.* She may not be the world's greatest singer, but credit where it's due, she does a proper line in put-downs.

4. **Louise Redknapp**

One of the original members of pre-Spice Girls-biggest-girl-group-in-the-world, Eternal, Louise Nurding married England and Liverpool player Jamie Redknapp in 1998. Injury deprived Jamie of large chunks of his career, but at least his wife was voted Sexiest Female of the Decade by readers of *FHM* magazine in 2004, which must be a compensation of sorts.

5. **Patsy Kensit**

Patsy boggled the nation's mind by having an affair with Scotland's top post-war scorer (415 in all competitions) and Glasgow Rangers legend, Ally McCoist. In his turn McCoist boggled the nation's mind once more when it was revealed that he had not *one* but *two* mistresses, the other being an air hostess, all of this unbeknownst to each other, notwithstanding the wife. Kensit infuriated one of her exes, Liam Gallagher, by bringing up their son Lennon as a Manchester United fan. Gallagher is famously vocal in his support of United's rivals, Manchester City. Now that *is* revenge.

6. Linda Evangelista

The supermodel who wouldn't get out of bed for less than $10,000 a day at the height of super-modelling in the '80s later shared a flat in Manchester with accident-prone French lunatic and Man United goalkeeper Fabien Barthez. As the hotel porter famously asked George Best as he cavorted about with Miss World in a sea of champagne on a bed strewn with casino winnings, 'Fabien, where did it all go wrong?'

Fabien Barthez: where did it all go wrong?

NATURAL PHENOMENA
DID HE REALLY MEAN TO DO THAT?

MY UNLUCKIEST EVER DAY
By **Paul Bennett**

MY UNLUCKIEST EVER DAY
by unlucky Coventry City fan, **Paul Bennett**

In 1987 Coventry achieved their greatest moment to date by reaching the FA Cup Final. It was a mouth-watering clash between the David of Coventry City and the Goliath of Tottenham Hotspur. Tickets were hard to come by and it was only by queuing all night long, with receipts from the other qualifying matches, that my brother was able to secure the prized dockets that would gain entry to Wembley. He managed to get one for himself, and another for his younger 10-year-old brother, me.

John Motson is on record as saying that it was one of the all-time great finals, a view shared by many other independent and non-partisan football followers. So imagine then if you were a Coventry fan (I know it's depressing, but bear with me) and your team is actually for the first time in their 104–year history about to achieve their greatest feat: of actually playing and matching a Spurs side, including eight England internationals (and an Argie!). Imagine a game filled with drama, skill (yes I am still talking about Coventry), passion and humour. Imagine you are actually there and you witness Keith Houchen flying through the air to connect with a Dave Bennett cross to score one of the most amazing diving headers ever to bring us back into the match for a second time, after going an initial goal down in just six minutes. Imagine going mental for the extra-time winner, the shot that deflected in off Gary Mabbutt's knee (a deflection that inspired a whole Coventry fanzine titled

Gary Mabbutt's Knee) – to make the final score Coventry 3–2 Spurs. Imagine you are there with tears in your eyes as that lovable giant, the mullet-permed, moustachioed warrior Brian Kilcline lifts the cup above his head screaming CITY! Imagine it for a second, even if you were not a football fan, imagine the sense of history, it would be like being present at the moon landing, or the fall of the Berlin Wall.

Only that's all I'll ever be able to do you see – imagine – because just before half-time I felt a sudden sharp pain on the lower right-hand side of my stomach. I tried to ignore it, but soon I was doubled up in pain, causing alarm all around me. My body had decided that this was the perfect place and time to have a little drama of its own – my appendix had chosen this very moment to grow to the size of a small water melon. I missed the rest of the match as, accompanied by my poor, resentful, still-not-over-it-even-to-this-very-day, brother, I was rushed to the nearest hospital. The only way I'll ever be able to make it up to him, of course, is if Coventry ever make it to another FA Cup Final … So, just another eighty or so years to go then.

If you ever watch the video you can see me being passed over the heads of the Coventry fans to the St John Ambulance men at the front.

10
GOALKEEPERS WHO HAVE SCORED

WHEN the situation looks dire and you're into the ninety-third minute with relegation staring you in the face, caution is thrown to the wind as the 'keeper steps forward to create havoc in the box for that last-gasp corner-kick moment of glory – like drummers in bands, they all dream of being the lead singer.

1. **Jimmy Glass**

   In the most last-gasp of all last gasps, Jimmy became a footballing legend when he scored the winning goal in the *ninety-fifth* minute of injury time of the final match of the 1998–99 season, thus saving Carlisle United from relegation and also enabling them to remain in the Football League (at the expense of Scarborough). Jimmy is immortalised in the Cumbrian city despite having only played with United for *three weeks* as an on-loan keeper. Just to demonstrate what ruthless bastards football chairmen are, his contract was not extended.

2. **José Luis Chilavert**

   Paraguay's unquestioned team leader, Chilavert is as vociferous and outrageous as he is reliable in his role as custodian between the goalposts. In 1998 he captured the attention of the world's sporting press after curling a free-kick around the wall and past his opposite number during an International against Argentina in Buenos Aires. A free-kick and penalty-shot specialist, Chilavert has over 50 goals to his credit – including eight for the national team. In 1999 he became the first goalkeeper to score a hat-trick in the history of the game, for Velez Sarsfield against Ferro Carril Oeste.

3. **Peter Schmeichel**

   Schmeichel scored 13 goals in his long and distinguished career, including one International goal for Denmark. Schmeichel headed Manchester United's equaliser from a corner in an UEFA Cup Tie against Rotor Volgograd in 1996, but United went out on the Away Goal rule. Blessed with a goal-scoring record that would shame a number of outfield players, Schmeichel's last effort was not enough to save Aston Villa when they lost to Everton 3–2 in the 2001/02 season.

4. Charlie Williams

The first recorded instance of a goalkeeper scoring direct from a goal-kick was on 14th April 1900 when Manchester City's Williams beat his opposite number, JE Doig, in the Sunderland goal.

5. Pat Jennings

Arguably the most famous goal of all time by a 'keeper was Jennings' effort in the 1967 Charity Shield while playing for Spurs against Manchester United. His goal clearance flew past his opposite number Alex Stepney after being caught by a gust of wind. The whole incident was caught by Match of the Day cameras and is repeated almost as often as the Morecambe and Wise Christmas special.

6. Paul Robinson

Leeds United's 'keeper scored a last-minute equaliser against Swindon Town in the Carling Cup in September 2003. Having sent the game into extra time, Robinson then saved a penalty in the shoot-out to win the game for the Yorkshire club.

7. Eric Viscaal

Viscaal, a Belgian outfield player, was forced to take over in goal during a clash between AA Ghent and Lokeren in 1994 after Ghent's regular keeper was sent off. His first act was to save a penalty, and then, with seconds to go, Ghent were awarded a penalty and Eric duly went up the other end and heroically scored.

8. **Bruce Grobbelaar**

The Liverpool 'keeper and Zimbabwe International netted a spot kick in 1980 in a game against York City while playing for Crewe Alexandra. Later to become famous for his jelly-legs gamesmanship (as emulated for Liverpool by Jerzy Dudek in the 2005 Champion's League penalty shoot-out), on this occasion Grobbelaar did the 'reverse-Bruce' by telling his opposite number exactly where he was going to place his spot kick.

9. **Roberto Bonano & José Luis Chilavert & José Luis Chilavert (again)**

Prior to 1912, goalkeepers regularly appeared on the score sheet thanks to rules that allowed them to handle the ball up to the halfway line. It was under these rules that two opposing goalkeepers both scored in the same match (Third Lanark vs Motherwell, 1910), the only time such a feat has ever occurred in a first class fixture until 2nd August 2000, when Velez Sarsfield's José Luis Chilavert (who else?) and River Plate's Roberto Bonano both netted from the penalty spot in a Copa Mercosur tie.

10. **Bobby Moore**

England legend Moore scored twice for the national side in 108 appearances. He once saved a penalty when he went in goal for West Ham in a League Cup semi-final replay in 1972. Moore parried the spot-kick from Stoke City's Mike Bernard, but Bernard followed up and netted the rebound, taking Stoke to Wembley for the first time since they were formed over a hundred years earlier. Founders of the football League, the Potters won the final 2–1, against Chelsea. To this day, the League Cup remains their only prestigious piece of silverware.

12 FASHION DISASTERS

Are they designed by living designers with a big flouncy qualification in designing garments, or do alien football gods hijack a first-year graphic design student and beam his creations into club shops in the dead of night?

1. *Hull*'s 1992/3 'tiger' kit. Inspired by car seat covers for a Ford Granada.

2. *AEK Athens*: in the 1998/99 season the Greek side dispensed with their yellow and black stripes in place of a monstrosity featuring a huge black double-headed eagle – the club's logo – splashed across the front. Very Goth.

3. *Everton*'s mid-'90s salmon-pink. Juventus made this mistake too. FACT: pink is not a colour to wear while playing football.

4. *Wales*'s new millennium skintight red. Whereas six-packed Italian demi-gods can get away with this style, John Hartson cannot.

5. *Stoke City*'s 1980s pin stripe 'Ricoh'. Was supposed to be red, but the dye used was so cheap it turned out orange: one wash and it bled to pink.

6. *Norwich City*'s mid '90s yellow & green 'broccoli and parsley sauce vomit' design.

7. *Sheffield Wednesday*'s 'Chupa Chups'. It doesn't matter how nice a shirt is, you'll always ruin it by plastering a yellow & red logo for a Spanish lollipop on the front, especially one designed by Salvador Dali (true fact: in 1969 the surrealist took time out from painting melting watches and burning giraffes to create the Chupa Chups lollipop logo).

8. *Derby County*'s inaugural kit replicated the colours of the county cricket club (who founded DCFC), and who saw it as a way of cashing in on the game's popularity to boost their own finances; the 1884 side therefore turned out in a chocolate, amber and pale-blue strip. Derby, who seem to be specialists in this category, tried out a Third Division away kit in the mid-'80s which was described by a local radio commentator as their 'Moulin Rouge tarts' outfit'.

9. *Coventry*'s 1978 chocolate-brown away strip with cream 'piping'. Winner of an Internet poll for worst shirt of all time. Looked good with a mullet. Not.

10. *Man United*'s 1995/6 hide-and-seek grey.

11. *Bristol Rovers* enjoyed five minutes of fame as they alarmed the country by decking themselves out in blinding tangerine and lemon quarters in the 1987/88 season.

12. The self-designed goalkeeper shirts of *Jorge Campos*. What's the Mexican for 'You're looking sharp, Jorge?' Think bad jockey silks and you're still nowhere near the awful reality.

And the winner is: no contest, it has to be the tiger

THE WALLFLOWER AWARD FOR THE MOST INVISIBLE SHIRT OF ALL TIME

A fashion decision was made by kit designers in the mid-'90s, and it was this: that fans would like nothing more than to be seen sporting a cool grey shirt bearing their club's crest because it would look so groovy with a pair of Levis. The England team were supplied with an Umbro shirt of redoubtable greyness for a short time, but the experiment found its nadir one sunny afternoon, in April, 1996. Man United, kitted out in their own new grey away shirts, found themselves 3–0 down to Southampton at half-time at The Dell. They came out for the second half in their third kit, a highly visible, blue/white. The reason given for the costume change, and the first half performance, by Alex Ferguson in the post-match interview was that the players were 'struggling to identify each other' in the shirts, which, ironically, had the sponsor's name 'Viewcam' plastered across the front. Not that the new shirts helped them much: even once they could see each other with absolute clarity they still lost the match 3–1, only scoring the consolation goal in the last minute.

LURCH XI

Kevin James   6' 07"
Nickname: le Freak
(Perth; Defender)

Tor Hogne Aaroy   6' 07"
Nickname: Tiny
(Aalesund, Norwegian Premier League; Forward)

Kevin Francis   6' 07"
Nickname: God
(Stockport County and others; Forward)

Jan Koller   6' 06"
Nickname: Tiny
(Borussia Dortmund, Czech Republic; Forward)

Kostas Chalkias   6' 05"
Nickname: Clanger
(Portsmouth, Greece; Goalkeeper)

Peter Crouch   6' 05"
Nickname: Shorty
(Liverpool and England; Forward)

Zat Knight   6' 05"
Nickname: The Outhouse
(Fulham; Defender)

Niall Quinn   6' 04"
Nickname: The Roof Inspector
(Arsenal, Man City, Sunderland,
Republic of Ireland; Forward)

Martin 'Tiny' Taylor   6' 04"
Nickname: (you guessed it)
(Blackburn, Birmingham; Defender)

Willem Van Der Ark   **6′ 03″**
Nickname: The Ark
(Cambuur, Leeuwarden, FC Utrecht, Aberdeen, Willem II,
GVAV, Rapiditas; Forward)

Tore Andre Flo   **6′ 03″**
Nickname: Flonaldo
(Chelsea, Rangers, Sunderland, Norway; Forward)

Height information taken largely from team and player websites.

TINY XI

If you're a titch, the good news would seem to be that
shortness is no impediment to travel, and that while you're
on your world tour it might well be worth your while popping
in for a trial at Tottenham Hotspur.

Leon Knight   **5′ 05″**
Brighton (Forward)

Paul Dickov   **5′ 05″**
Blackburn (Forward)

Dennis Wise   **5′ 06″**
Southampton (Midfield)

Paul McVeigh   **5′ 06″**
Spurs and Norwich (Forward)

Shaun Wright-Philips   **5′ 06″**
Chelsea (Wing)

Gianfranco Zola   **5' 06"**
Chelsea, Cagliari (Forward)

Osvald Ardiles (Ossie)   **5' 07"**
Huracán, **Spurs**, Paris St Germain, **Spurs**, Blackburn
Rovers, Swindon Town (Midfield)

Jermain Defoe   **5' 07"**
West Ham, **Spurs** (Forward)

Andy Reid   **5 '07"**
Forest, **Spurs** (Midfield)

Jimmy Greaves   **5' 08"**
AC Milan, **Spurs** (Forward)

Robbie Keane   **5' 08"**
Coventry, Inter, Leeds, **Spurs** (Forward)

*Lack of height information taken largely from team and player
websites.*

TWITCHER'S 10

There are many species of bird to be found at football
grounds, here are some of them:

1. Bridled Tern

Easily the rarest species seen at a UK football ground
– with only 18 sightings in British waters the Bridled
Tern is more at home in the tropical seas of the Pacific,
Caribbean and Indian Ocean. Which makes it all the
more remarkable that one should show up at Arbroath
Football Club, Angus and Dundee, in July, 2003.

2. **Ryukyu Serpent-Eagle**

Spotted during England vs Brazil, June 2002 World Cup at Shizuoka Stadium, Japan.

3. **Northern Parula**

Spotted on 'The Garrison' on St Mary's, Isle of Scilly, during a Birdwatchers vs Islanders match, October 1987.

4. **Four Northern Long-tailed Tits**

Seen beside the toilet block at Lewes Football Club, Sussex, on 31st January 2004.

5. **Waxwing**

The Britannia Stadium, Staffordshire, February 2005.

6. **Black Kite**

Home Park, Plymouth, Devon, April 2004.

7. **Barn Owl**

Spotted at Ashton Gate, Bristol City, Gloucestershire. It must have been roosting in the roof of the stand, and as the ground started to fill with fans and the noise levels increased, it flew the length of the pitch and over the stand at the far end of the ground. Magnificent sight.

8. **Mute Swan**

June 2004. Seen flying over the City of Manchester Stadium, Greater Manchester, Lancs, during the England vs Iceland game.

9. **Iceland Gulls**

Thousands of gulls fly over White Hart Lane as they head for their roosts on the King George V and William Girling reservoirs in Stanwell and Edmonton, Middlesex.

10. XI Headless Chickens

Appear all over the country every Saturday afternoon.

Thanks to Dr Graham Etherington for information and research on this one.

OCEAN'S XI

Bert Trautmann

Mike Salmon   John Scales   Stern John   Andy Flounders

Wade Elliot   Mark Fish   Paul Mariner

Mark Ferry   Geoff Pike   Peter Haddock

10 CULT HEROES AND LOCAL LEGENDS

1. **Alex Calvo Garcia** for Scunthorpe United

   Garcia brought a little Spanish sunshine and lingo to North Lincs. On arriving in 1996 he was asked by a Radio Humberside interviewer how Scunthorpe compared to his home town in Spain. His response? 'Ahh ... the laydeeezz of Scunthorpe, very nice, I like a lot.' Asked to summarise his eight years with the club on his return to Spain in 2004, Alex said: 'I have lived the most exciting years of my life here, I'm proud of what I did. I wouldn't change anything, if I had to live the last eight years again I would come straight away to Scunthorpe.'

2. **Paul McGrath** for Aston Villa

   A legendary defender who routinely missed out on training sessions and international matches through drinking bouts, McGrath had eight operations on knees that were notorious for being dodgy. Notwithstanding these difficulties, he more than made up for his lack of pace and declining fitness with a superb ability to read the game. He would be unlikely to cope with the speed and all-round fitness that typifies the sport in the new millennium, but neither could anybody else whose entire training regime consisted of anything up to one whole hour a week on a cycling machine. McGrath earned the PFA Player of the Year award in 1993.

3. **Lex 'Lexy' Grant** for Stranraer

   Turned out at Stair Park in the '80s and '90s. Overweight, lazy, glory-hunting, but blessed with a certain talent if the mood took him. Apparently he could pick a ball out of nowhere to turn a game, but his biggest pleasure in life came in hanging out on the wing and chatting to the crowd. Here may be the reason why he never made it to the big time.

4. **Dariusz 'Jacki' Dziekanowski** for Bristol City

'He may be from a different country ... today he's been from a different planet.' This was commentator John Motson's assessment of Dziekanowski's contribution to Bristol's 3–0 FA Cup win against Leicester City in 2001. With 60-odd Poland caps to his credit, Jacki joined Bristol from Celtic in 1992. Some say he was the last of the international playboys, while others say he made Gazza look like a born-again teetotaller – the consensus of opinion being that this is how he found himself at a club like Bristol City. When he left, he became a plumber in Warsaw. Somehow we don't imagine there's much chance of him turning up to fix a leak when he says he will.

5. **Derek Dawkins** for Torquay United

Scored the single goal at Plainmoor which famously put Tottenham out of the League Cup in the mid-'80s. But never mind that, 'The Dude' was widely regarded as 'the coolest man in Torquay'. Top that.

6. **Steve Foster** for Brighton and Hove Albion

Noted for his trademark headband, Foster was a colossus at the back for the Seagulls. As Brighton captain he was desperately disappointed to miss the FA Cup final in 1983 against Manchester United in which the south-coast team (who were relegated from the top flight in the same season) pulled off an unexpected 2–2 draw after extra time. This meant a replay, for which Foster was declared fit. But Brighton could not repeat the heroics of the first encounter, going down to a 4–0 scoreline. To help cheer him up, Manchester United supporters sang, *'Steven Foster, Steven Foster, what a difference you have made, what a diff-er-ence you have made'*.

7. **Neville Southall** for Everton

One of the best goalkeepers in the world, who won League, FA, and Cup Winners' Cup medals, Big Nev's exceptional ability between the sticks was only surpassed by his exceptional unwillingness to smile. Win the Cup and have a celebratory party? Negative: scowl, leave your teammates to it, and drive yourself back to the missus in north Wales to spend a night in watching the box. In a Legends vs Celebrities match arranged by Channel 4 in 2005, Southall was notable for the disdain with which he parried the efforts of spotty young soap stars who entertained the preposterous notion of getting the ball past him.

8. **Roberto Martinez** for Wigan Athletic

'Bob' arrived at Springfield Park in a blaze of publicity in the summer of '95 alongside compatriots *Jesus Seba* and *Isidro Diaz*. Helping raise the profile of the club on its journey up the divisions and onto the Premiership, the Spanish trio were dubbed The Three Amigos, and while Seba didn't survive much more than a season, and Diaz often flattered to deceive, Martinez was the real thing. The clean-living model professional has a place in English football history as the first Spaniard ever to score in the FA Cup (against Runcorn, first round

'95/96). Spanish flags and sombreros appeared on the terraces, and 'Olé!' became a regular chant. If you've ever been to Wigan you'll know just what an extraordinary accomplishment Martinez achieved there.

9. **Steve Bull** for Wolves

Pound for pound the greatest striker to play for Wolverhampton Wanderers: at a cost of just £65,000, 'Bully' netted 306 times to shatter the club's goalscoring record; he chalked up 52 competitive goals in the '87/88 season alone, and 18 hat-tricks in his 13 seasons with the Black Country club. Bull represented England while playing in the old Third Division and remains a folk hero amongst all Wolves fans – the fact that one of the stands is named in his honour says it all. His long-term loyalty to Wolves is renowned. Though not quite a one-club man, his lengthy career with a single club is all but a thing of the past now.

10. **Rodney Marsh** for QPR

Acme of the '70s playboy who fitted in the odd game when he could find the time in between the birds, the bookies and the nightclubs, Marsh set the Bush alight. Blessed with skill, vision, cheek and good looks, Rodney will be remembered as an extrovert forward with an aversion to restricting himself to doing the expected – for instance the penalty he took against Ipswich when he ran

Rodney Marsh, keeping his ears open for the descending minor third

from the halfway line, swerving, jumping in the air, and looking as though he was pedalling a bike. He got to the ball and stopped, the goalie dived, and he rolled it into the other corner. Marsh was honoured with this Pseuds' Corner entry from composer Michael Nyman, writing in the *Guardian* in 2005:

> *I maintain that the best writing about QPR – and possibly about football – was a piece I commissioned from John Tilbury for* Vogue. *It was a musicological analysis of the descending minor third in the 'Rodney!' chant that QPR fans of the early '70s sang for Rodney Marsh, based on the differences in the chant when QPR were winning and when they were losing.*

10 TANNOY ANNOUNCEMENTS

1. Will Andrew Jones of Barnsley please contact the nearest steward. You've locked your mother out of the house.
   Norwich City vs Barnsley, 2001. This means, unfortunately for Mrs Jones, that she was locked out of her house 190 miles away from the person who had the key.

2. Port Vale! I've been rubbing my lamp all morning!
   Jack Wild, who played the Artful Dodger in the film Oliver, *appeared in panto – in Aladdin – in Stoke-on-Trent in the early '90s. He turned up at Vale Park, was introduced over the Tannoy, grabbed the mic, and shouted the above. Now there was a man who knew his audience.*

3. The special train leaves at 17:15 – for those of you from Merseyside that is quarter past five.
   Barnsley vs Everton, FA Cup, 1989.

4. Will the owner of a car, registration …, parked in the army barracks, please return to your vehicle immediately.

You will regret it if you don't.

5 minutes later:

Will the owner of a car, registration ..., please return to your vehicle in the next 2 minutes otherwise it will be blown up. You will know if you are too late – you will hear it.

This message was heard at Colchester United's Layer Road stadium, situated across the road from an army estate, in the early '80s, when the IRA was active in England.

5. We'd like to wish the travelling support a safe trip back to Division Two.

    Tranmere Rovers 0–2 QPR, 1996. The Rovers announcer gets his retaliation in following a reverse for the home side in the FA Cup. He was sacked, but later reinstated following a fans' protest. They have their followers, these voices in the ether. (See also **Last Words,** *no. 3, p.298)*

6. Pack up and clear off.

    Former Scotland coach Craig Brown recalls his time as manager of cash-strapped Clyde in the mid-'80s. When they were training on the pitch it wasn't unusual to hear this order booming out – because greyhound time-trials were about to start on the perimeter track. 'They didn't want us hitting the dogs with a stray ball; to be fair, most of the greyhounds had cost a hell of a lot more than my players,' said Brown.

7. i.   Can programme seller number 13 report to the office?

    ii. Can programme seller number 13 please report to the office?

    iii. Can programme seller number 13 PLEASE report to the office?

iv. Anyone knowing the whereabouts of programme seller number 13 please report to the office.

Barnsley vs Sheffield Wednesday, August, 1979. A report in the Sheffield Star three days after the game began: 'Missing programme seller number 13 (name), aged 14, has been found alive and well in Blackpool.' (Skint, of course.)

8. Scorer of the second goal for Bournemouth, number 2, Mark Newson. *Crowd boos.*

Okay, sorry: scorer of the second goal for Bournemouth, number 5, John Williams. *Crowd erupts in a world of heaven.*

Bournemouth vs Plymouth, New Year's day, 1990. Newson had advised he wanted a transfer out of the club, whereas Williams was a crowd favourite and everyone saw it deflect in off Williams' bonce, and everyone wanted to hear credit given where credit was due.

9. Congratulations to Mr. So-and-so from Hull ... your wife's given birth to a son.

Hull 0–1 Blackpool, 2001. This announcement is made at the end of an evening game played in freezing conditions. As they leave the ground, one Blackpool fan is heard to say to another, 'Poor sod ... his side's lost and now there's no-one at home to get his tea ready.'

10. *Early in first half:* Will Mr. So-and-so please contact the nearest steward – your wife has gone into labour.

Later in 1st half: Will Mr. So-and-so please contact the nearest steward – your wife has gone into hospital.

Early in 2nd half: Will Mr. So-and-so please contact the nearest steward – your wife is in hospital, and she's in labour.

Later in 2nd half: Will Mr. So-and-so never mind contacting the nearest steward – your wife has given birth to a baby boy!

Despite all the provocation, Mr. So-and-so remains at Burnden Park, Bolton, to see Barnsley win 3–2 away in the final fixture of the 1993/94 campaign. It was a meaningless encounter with neither side in any danger of either relegation or promotion. It becomes clear that Mr. So-and-so got his priorities right, however, when we discover that this was the only match during the whole season in which a Barnsley player scored more than once, and it was the only away game they won when the opposition also scored.

It may be noted from the above that the Yorkshire side, Barnsley FC, appear to be specialists in this category. Nobody knows why this is.

BEHAVIOUR
AND THE WILL
WHAT DOES HE USE FOR BRAINS?

FOOTBALL'S NOT JUST ABOUT SCORING
GOALS – IT'S ABOUT WINNING
By **John Street**

10 MISSILES

10 ANGELS

5 PLEAS FOR HELP (AND 79 EARLY BATHS)

15 RED CARDS

2 SENDINGS-OFF IN LESS THAN THE BLINK OF AN EYE

NAUGHTY XI

7 EXISTENTIAL CRISES

7 TRIUMPHS OVER ADVERSITY

MARCHING OFF TO WAR – THE 10 CLUBS THAT SENT
MOST MEN TO SERVICE IN WORLD WAR II

FOOTBALL'S NOT JUST ABOUT SCORING GOALS – IT'S ABOUT WINNING *

Professor of Politics **John Street** gets stuck in

Thomas Hobbes, the seventeenth-century political philosopher, believed that without the presence of an absolute authority – a leviathan – the life of man would be 'solitary, poor, nasty, brutish and short.' But then Hobbes had never seen the five-a-side games played every night on countless floodlit astroturf pitches: if these games may occasionally tend towards the brutal, it's nonetheless true that even without a referee – football's leviathan – ten (or so) men still manage to enjoy themselves without carnage and unnecessary loss of life. (*See also* **The Rules of 5-a-side**, p.288.)

Football has, though, acquired a reputation for, at best, its amorality, if not its immorality. With the diving, the bungs and the hands of god, the game has been portrayed as the progeny of a marriage of the Mafia and Borgias. It was football that gave us the 'professional foul', – in a television play of the same name, the eminent playwright Sir Tom Stoppard has one of his characters, a philosopher, pour scorn on the behaviour of players who simultaneously appeal for a throw-in, even when they know who touched it last: themselves. Stoppard's reactionary snobbery is matched by the Marxist disdain of Theodor Adorno, who with his usual cheery delight in modern society writes, 'Sport itself is not play but ritual in which the subjected celebrate their subjection. The rules of the game resemble those of the market, equal chances and fair play for all, but only as the struggle of all against all.' In short, football, capitalism, it's all the same; dog-eat-dog and the remains served up as pet food.

Only cricket, it seems, rises above the pit of depravity that is football. Where the beautiful game gives us the professional foul, cricket's bequest is the idea of 'gentlemanly conduct', of England's Andrew Flintoff consoling his vanquished rival, the Australian fast bowler Brett Lee. It is cricket that still harbours the ideal that batsmen should 'walk' if they are out, whatever the verdict of the umpire, that fielders should be taken at their word if they claim a catch. The reality, of course, is not like this. Cricketers – at least professional cricketers – no more walk than Manchester United 'keeper Roy Carroll admits that the ball was a yard over the line, with the goal not given. Cricketers have been found guilty of match-fixing, of ball-tampering, and of other behaviour that is simply 'not cricket'.

Cricket's moral virtues – the taking part, not the winning, the honourable draw – are the product of nineteenth-century aristocratic public schools. None of which stopped Marxists like CLR James and Paul Foot extolling the virtues of the game. But in hymning cricket's values, and decrying football's commercialism, they conveniently overlook Robbie Fowler's public support for striking Liverpool dockers or Inter Milan's Javier Zanetti persuading his teammates to donate money to the Zapatista rebels. And then, of course, there was Paolo Di Canio refusing a shooting opportunity and catching the ball instead, rather than taking what he saw as an unfair advantage.

The real issue, of course, is not cricket versus football, not the good versus the iniquitous. It is that team sport – all team sport – is an experiment in social order, and as such is dependent on shared moral values, shared within and between teams. The philosopher Martin Hollis wrote, 'Football, played in the right spirit, is a team game involving trust, obligations and a willingness to play fair.' A side of rampant individualists, in which everyone plays for themselves, would end up in the relegation zone. In mid-table would be the Kantians, who obey universal laws of duty that dictate when to pass and shoot. And at the top, the Brazil of the moral league, are those who take their instructions from the team and put the team first. Maybe it's a coincidence, but two of the greatest managers – Alex Ferguson and Brian Clough – have been socialists, not Thatcherites. If this is the key to winning, then it suggests that successful football needs a sophisticated moral code. And if this is the case, then the political scientist Lincoln Allison may be right when he says that sports clubs enable people 'to develop democratic skills, practices and values'. There are 40,000 football clubs in the UK.

* *Alan Shearer*

10
MISSILES

The tricky bit is concealing it inside your parka

1. A VESPA

Inter Milan supporters took a scooter into the ground after stealing it from an Atalanta fan during a pre-match scuffle in 2001. Photographs showed a group of fans trying to set the vehicle on fire before hurling it from an upper stand on to an empty section of the stadium. No one was injured in the incident.

2. A hand grenade

At Brentford on 6th November 1965 a hand grenade was hurled into the home team's penalty area in a match involving Millwall. It was launched following a Lions equaliser in a game they won 2–1. Insouciant Brentford 'keeper Chic Brodie picked it up, inspected it, and then tossed it into the net. PC Pat O'Connell removed it from the rigging, placed it in a handy bucket of sand and took it to the nearby station, where it was confirmed as a harmless dummy. Most people in the crowd were unaware of any commotion – and when they found out most commented that the match had been a dud too – but the Sunday papers went to town: 'Soccer Marches to War' was typical of the headlines.

3. An avalanche of origami

Play was temporarily held up when Brighton 'keeper Wayne Henderson's goal was bombarded by red and blue paper aeroplanes in a league match away to deadly rivals Crystal Palace in 2005.

4. Daffodils

In a tribute to Morrisey in the '80s QPR fans used to throw flowers at Les Sealey from the Loft while serenading him with a stereo chorus of 'Les Sealey is a homosexual'. No one knew whether there was any truth in this rumour but it scanned well and Sealey's steam-out-of-the-ears reaction made the exercise wholly worthwhile; 'Mr Angry', who did not earn his nickname for nothing and was the most easily wound-up player in the world.

5. **Celery**

   In the late '70s and early '80s Chelsea fans had a habit of nicking this versatile vegetable from allotments and making merry by launching sticks of it onto the pitch at Abbey Road, home of Cambridge United, when the two teams were in the old Second Division and animosities ran high.

6. **Tennis balls**

   In 1997, David Lloyd, captain of the Great Britain Davis Cup tennis team, and a successful businessman, became the owner of Hull City. For a variety of reasons – to do with a perception that he was even more useless at running a football club than those that went before him – Lloyd was vastly unpopular. His name remains a swear word on Humberside to this day and at the height of the protests that developed in response to his regime, fans took to throwing tennis balls onto the pitch. The most memorable occasion was at Bolton's Reebok Stadium during a cup tie when hundreds of them were launched onto the pitch from the vantage point of a high upper-tier location for away fans.

7. **Bottles filled with urine**

   Along with stones, these unsanitary cocktails formed part of a barrage that saw the death of two people in the war-torn Liberian capital of Monrovia after fans went on the rampage during a 2004 World Cup group game between Liberia and Senegal. Liberia's football executives denounced the violence saying, 'These people are hiding behind the football game to achieve their goals. They are not Lone Star [Liberia's nickname] fans. They are hooligans, mere looters who were waiting for the match to execute their plans.' Whatever those plans were, they failed to piss off the Lions of Senegal, who won the match 3–0.

8. A plethora of upholstery

At Sheffield Wednesday in the late '70s and early '80s supporters used to be able to buy cushions for the hard wooden seats. Occasionally (and only naturally) one or two cushions would end up on the field of play. A poor spell that nearly sent the Yorkshire club into the bottom division saw the entire North Stand express their disgust at the state of the world in general, and the sending off of David 'Bronco' Layne in particular, as, during a fixture against Aston Villa, hundreds of cushions were hurled onto the pitch simultaneously, causing the game to be delayed. There was trouble from the FA and a warning was issued, leading ultimately to an outright ban of the comfy seating arrangements.

9. A large amount of ironmongery

Following a 1999 Cannes vs Nice derby clash, Cannes goalkeeper Sebastien Chabbert was left under observation in hospital after being struck on the head by a missile thrown from the Nice fans behind his goal. As Chabbert lay on the ground clutching his head a firework exploded next to him – he suffered concussion and temporary loss of memory. Cannes walked off after the 84th-minute incident and the match was abandoned (Nice were leading 1–0). Objects thrown onto the pitch included two pairs of scissors, iron bars, stones, fireworks, two mobile telephones and a solid lead ball used in the French game of pétanque.

10. **The curious incident of the boomeranging bottle of water**

Millwall 'keeper Tony Warner got his career off to a dream start after South Wales Police charged him on two counts relating to an incident during the opening day fixture of the 1999/2000 season at Cardiff City. Warner was charged with causing actual bodily harm after allegedly throwing a bottle into the crowd, one that had initially been launched onto the pitch by the Cardiff fans.

10 ANGELS

1. **Bill 'Dixie' Dean**

The Everton legend once claimed the only thing he ever received from a referee was a boiled sweet. In 502 first-class games he notched up zero sendings off and no bookings. Dixie scored 60 League goals in the 1927/28 season, in which Everton won the Division One title, a record that remains unsurpassed. His nickname is said to have been given to him by fans due to his dark complexion and curly black hair, which was, in their perception, similar to that of African-Americans in the southern United States. Dean deeply disliked the moniker, preferring to be known as Bill.

2. **Tommy Lawton**

Another Goodison great who created a sensation in 1947 when he joined Third Division Notts County while still England's first-choice centre forward, for a new record transfer fee of £20,000. He was never booked or sent off in a 20-year professional career taking in 390 league games and 23 full internationals. He astonished the County crowd with his goalscoring exploits – 103 in 166 appearances – and also created a new record by becoming the first Third Division footballer to be capped by England: he won four of his England caps as a County player.

3. **Gary Lineker**

Mr Clean is yet another ambassador of fair play to have passed through Goodison Park. In a career that took in over 450 games at Leicester, Everton, Barcelona, Spurs and Nagoya Grampus Eight – not forgetting 80 caps for England – Lineker's name never once appeared in the referee's book.

4. **Sir Stanley Matthews**

Known as the *The First Gentleman of Football*, Sir Stan's exemplary sportsmanship took in a career covering around 700 games for Stoke City, Blackpool and England which saw him go entirely without caution. At 42 years and 104 days he became the oldest player ever to receive an England cap: vs Denmark in Copenhagen on May 15, 1957. In 1965 Stanley Matthews became the first professional footballer to be knighted.

5. **Sir Tom Finney**

Apparently the winger was never even *spoken* to by an official in all his years with Preston, the hometown team for whom he played out his entire league career, which took in 433 games in which he scored 187 times. Known as a one-man team (there was a joke that went: Tom Finney should claim income tax relief ... for his 10 dependents) he never won a major club honour, this from a player who notched up 30 goals in his 76 England appearances. In a curious episode, in 1963, a few years after retirement, Finney played a one-off in the home leg of a European cup-tie for Distillery: at the behest of Distillery manager George Eastham, and at the age of 41, he captained the Irish side to a 3–3 draw against Benfica.

The Splash, Tom Finney. Sports Photograph of the Year, 1956.
A statue based on this image – taken at a match between Chelsea and Preston – was unveiled outside the National Football Museum, Deepdale, in 2004.

6. Billy Wright

Wing-half William Ambrose Wright was the first and most exemplary player to record 100 England caps. Keeping his nose clean during the whole of 541 games for Wolves, and a total 105 for England, Wright's England career was hugely distinguished: he captained his country in 90 matches, a world record that he shares with Bobby Moore; he played for his country in a world record 70 successive matches, all as captain; and he captained his country at a record three World Cup final tournaments, in 1950, 1954 and 1958.

7. John Charles

Beginning at Swansea, the Welsh hero's career spanned 18 years and took him to Leeds United – where the 42 goals he scored in the 1953–54 season remains a club record – and then to Juventus in 1957 for a record transfer fee of £67,000. The Juve fans anointed him *Il Buono Gigante* – The Gentle Giant. His nickname was well-earned: noted around the world for his sporting conduct, Charles was another who never troubled a referee's notebook.

8. **Jimmy Dickinson**

'Gentleman Jim' made 812 appearances for Portsmouth and England between 1946 and 1965 without so much a stern stare from an official. The left-half played 764 league games for Pompey – a record for one player at a single club until Swindon's John Trollope surpassed it in 1980, finishing on 770 appearances.

9. **William 'Billy' Liddell**

Spotted while playing for Lochgelly Violet at the age of 15, the Scottish winger/forward spent his entire professional career at Anfield scoring 229 goals in 537 matches for Liverpool during the late '40s and through the '50s. He was so pre-eminent in the side that for a time the crowd paid him the compliment of calling the team 'Liddellpool'.

10. **Eddie Gray**

Left winger in the infamous ruffian Leeds team of the late '60s and '70s, the side that included the likes of Norman 'bites yer legs off' Hunter. Amazingly, in 18 years as a player at Leeds between (1965–1983) he was never booked or sent off. 'We had enough players in our side who could take care of that side of things,' he said. Quite.

5 PLEAS FOR HELP
(AND 79 EARLY BATHS)

1. **Roy 'Donut' McDonough** – 21 red cards

   The midfield cruncher and Southend cult always gave 150 per cent and usually displayed two full sets of studs while he was at it.

2. **Willie Johnston** – 21 red cards

   It's a law of football that red-haired Scots must always be described as 'fiery'. Former international Johnston was no exception, taking seven fiery early walks while playing for West Bromwich Albion alone.

3. **Steve Walsh** – 13 red cards

   The Leicester City hard man was your typical committed crowd-pleasing defender, the type that home fans adore and away fans despise. Described as being a 'red rag to a Steve Bull' for his notorious running battle with his regular Wolverhampton opponent, Walsh was also banned for 11 matches following a nasty incident with David Geddis which left the Shrewsbury player with a broken jaw on the opening day of the 1987/88 season.

4. **Mark Dennis** – 12 red cards

   The former Southampton left-back would have done much better in his career were it not for his pathological hatred of referees.

5. **Dennis Wise** – 12 red cards

   After spells at Chelsea and Leicester, Wise took a player-manager post with Millwall in October 2003 (having joined the club as a player in September 2002). In his first game in charge, Millwall beat Sheffield United 2–0 but Wise was sent off just four minutes after bringing himself on as a substitute. Loved and loathed in equal measure, Wise demonstrates classic 'short man syndrome' – a loudmouth, cheeky, show-off, irritant – always jumping up and down, causing a fuss and generally being a pain in the arse.

15 RED CARDS

The most dismissals in a single English League match is a shared record:

5: Wigan (Jones) vs Bristol Rovers (Perry, Prichard, Tillson, Low), 2nd December 1997

Of the five players sent off in this match, three went from Bristol Rovers just before half-time, as well as Jones from Wigan. Unsurprisingly Wigan won 3–0, though they didn't get the last 2 goals until Rovers had Low dismissed on 71 minutes and were down to 7.

5: Chesterfield (Carr, Davies) v Plymouth (Jones, Logan, Mauge), 22nd February 1997

Plymouth's Jones was sent off for a two-footed challenge; the other four were sent off following a 22–man brawl in the final minute, instigated by Bruce Grobbelaar who pretended to have been injured by the shy and retiring Darren Carr.

5: Exeter (Cronin, Miller, Sheldon) vs Cambridge (Tudor, Youngs), 23rd November 2002

Another day, another last-minute mêlée. They were all

sent off in the 93rd minute. Five sendings-off in injury time is a record too.

(Note the lower league nature of these three fixtures. You get all the riff-raff down there.)

2 SENDINGS-OFF IN LESS THAN THE BLINK OF AN EYE

Recorded as zero seconds:

1. Ian Banks, Bournemouth v Barnsley, 16th December 1989

   Banks was sent off for giving a linesman the benefit of his opinion regarding an offside decision that went against his team while warming up to come on as a substitute. The linesman called the ref over, and the red card was shown.

2. Walter Boyd, Swansea v Darlington, 23rd November 1999

   Boyd came on as substitute for Swansea during a break in play. The stoppage was to allow referee Clive Wilkes to send off Darlington's Steve Tutill, for a foul. By the time Wilkes turned around from completing the dismissal, Darlington's Martin Gray was lying face down clutching his head. The linesman advised the ref that Boyd had elbowed Gray in the face while making his way onto the pitch (there was later an accusation from Boyd of a racist remark by Gray). The Jamaican was sent off before play had a chance to re-start.

NAUGHTY XI

1. Peter Shilton

Shilton was arrested for drink-driving in 1980 after being found in a country lane with a woman called Tinà in his car at 5am. Tina's husband Colin somehow arrived on the scene to find the pair partially clothed. Shilton hurriedly drink-drove away and crashed into a lamppost. He admitted to 'taking a lady for a meal' and was fined £350 and banned from driving for 15 months. This sort of activity is going to cause trouble for any player. *Peter Shilton, Peter Shilton, Does your missus know you're here?* is quite a mild song to have sung to you in the circumstances, probably reflecting the widespread affection in which the long-serving (125 caps) England 'keeper was held.

2. Dennis Wise

Him again. If ever a chirpy little 'character' deserved widespread disapprobation from the terraces, you'd have to say that Dennis Wise is that man. On Leicester's 2003 pre-season tour to Finland, Wise and a number of other Leicester teammates were playing cards in Callum Davidson's room. Davidson wanted to go to sleep so asked them to leave. Wise wouldn't depart, and an argument ensued. It ended with a number of players removing Wise bodily from Davidson's room. Later, when everyone had gone to sleep, brave little Wisey went back into the room and attacked his teammate while he slept, leaving Davidson with a fractured cheekbone.

3. Peter Beagrie

On Everton's 1991 pre-season tour of Spain Beagrie

went on a night out following a game with Real Sociedad. In the early hours he flagged down a Spanish motorcyclist, who gave him a lift. On arriving at his hotel Beagrie couldn't wake the night porter, so he commandeered the Spaniard's bike and rode it up the hotel steps and straight through a plate glass window. Only it was the wrong hotel. Beagrie required just the 50 stitches. Dangerous idea, the pre-season tour.

4. **Bertie Auld**

In a 1963 match at St Andrews, Birmingham winger Auld was fouled by Fulham's Johnny Haynes. Auld, who was legendary for his temper, knocked out Haynes in retaliation. He then flattened another Fulham player who tried to intervene, rendering him unconscious as well. Both Auld and Haynes were sent off, the latter on a stretcher.

5. **Julian Alsop**

'Striker banned for lewd banana prank' read the headlines in January 2005 as former Oxford United striker Julian Alsop was barred from playing until the end of the season by the Football Association. The player had already been sacked after the club found out that he'd committed a 'bizarre act' on a younger player on the training ground. Some reports had alleged that he'd tried to stick a banana somewhere where it should not go. Training sessions must get quite boring though, and need an occasional bit of livening up.

6. **Mickey Thomas**

Sentenced to prison for counterfeiting currency in 1993, Thomas was born to spend time doing lines in

detention (*I must not forge banknotes* a hundred times).
The prevailing image of the long-haired winger was the
one that went out for many years on the *Match of the Day*
opening credits. He is caught writhing around the pitch
in agony following a rough challenge, until he realises
the cameras are on him, at which point he perks up no
end and brazenly winks at the watching millions. Back
down to your desk Thomas, and write out a thousand
times: I must not feign injury, I must not feign injury,
I must not feign injury … (He'd be bound to bring his
own printing press.)

7. **Robin Friday**

The most charismatic Welshman ever to wear a Reading
shirt, Friday was signed by manager Charlie Hurley
after starring for Hayes against Reading in an FA Cup
tie. He scored twice on his home debut for the Royals
in a 4–1 win against Exeter City. A sort of prototype
Gazza, Friday was frequently to be found in the Spread
Eagle pub next to the ground until about ten minutes
before kick-off. While he was still at Hayes they started
one game with ten men because he was finishing off a
pint (or several). Apparently he was pissed as a newt
and spent the match staggering around the pitch being
ignored by the opposition – until, that is, he scored the
only goal of the game. In 1974 he took a crap in the
opposition's bath after he was sent off at Elm Park. Just
after his transfer from Reading to Cardiff in 1976 he was
arrested at the station when he tried travelling with only
a platform ticket once too often. When he died at the
age of 38 in 1990 it was to no one's particular surprise
that it was from a drug-induced heart attack.

8. Paul Gascoigne

Could fill a volume of his own for naughtiness, and another more substantial tome for stupidity. One of the few players to model himself on Norman Wisdom, a couple of 'classic' Gazza 'pranks' are the one where he walked into the Middlesbrough canteen and ordered lunch wearing nothing but his training socks (excuse us while we split our sides), and the other one where he booked a series of sun-bed sessions for then-Newcastle teammate Tony Cunningham, who is of course, black. The tears are rolling down our faces at the memory. And didn't he once substitute cat poo for mincemeat in Christmas pies? Oooeer missus, stop!

9. The Manchester City squad

Silly more than naughty, the lads were denied entry into a nightclub during the 1999 Christmas party because they were, to a man, dressed as Harry Enfield-type Scousers.

10. Taribo West

The defender was sacked from Kaiserslautern for calling in sick for a league match and then flying to Milan to attend his own birthday party. Capped 40 times for the 'Super Eagles' of Nigeria, West is rightly famous for sporting green dreadlock topknots, a very naughty hairstyle whichever way you cut it.

Naughty boy, naughty hair

11. **Chokri El Ouaer**

In the African Champions League final in December 2000 in the Ghanaian city of Accra between Hearts of Oak and Esperance of Tunisia, Esperance 'keeper Chokri El Ouaer cut himself above the eye in an attempt to get the game abandoned.

In a riotous atmosphere, as the crowd pelted the linesman with an assortment of objects and tear gas was fired into the crowd, a small group of travelling Tunisian fans scaled the fences to seek refuge. During the mêlée, a supporter ran on to the pitch and handed El Ouaer an object with which he cut a gash on the side of his face. The 'keeper (who played at the World Cup finals in France in 1998) ran to the centre of the field with blood streaming from the wound, and collapsed at the halfway line. But both the referee and linesman had seen the incident and the only result was that he had to leave the pitch injured. Esperance inexplicably brought on an outfield player and put midfielder Hassen Gabsi in goal, leaving reserve goalkeeper Mohamed Zouabi on the bench. Hearts quickly scored three goals to secure the continent's flagship club trophy 5–2 on aggregate. (Which means that the game was all square when Chokri had his great idea and his sudden rush of blood.)

Naughty XI Coach. **Steve Harrison**

The Millwall first team coach was sacked in 1991 for perching on top of a wardrobe in a hotel room and, in a re-enactment of a *Viz* routine, aiming a turd into a pint glass on the floor. It seems possible that alcohol may have been involved.

Naughtie XI Mascot. **Freddie the Fox**

Freddie was banned from Rochdale FC in 2001 for behaving a bit like a fox. Freddie, the Halifax mascot, was told to stay away from Spotland following an incident in which he cocked his leg against a goal post. Desmond the Dragon, the Rochdale mascot, saw red at the slight and dived in and started a brawl. A club official confirmed that Freddie had been banned for starting it, saying, 'Desmond *is* quite a fiery character, but whatever he's done I'm sure it's not as bad as shitting in a pint pot from the top of a wardrobe.'

7 EXISTENTIAL CRISES

1. Marco Boogers

'Not like it said in the brochure,' was Harry Redknapp's verdict on the player he signed for £1 million from Sparta Rotterdam for West Ham in 1995.

In Redknapp's autobiography, *'Arry*, he describes the situation as it unfolded. Right from the word go his attitude stank ... all the players disliked him, he hated training, his wife couldn't settle ... in his first game against Man United the only kick he had was the one he slung at Gary Neville that got him sent off. He was declared "psychologically unfit" for football – which only meant he'd persuaded a doctor to come up with some excuse why he couldn't return – and disappeared somewhere back home.'

Boogers was discovered several weeks after this episode hiding in a mobile home in a Dutch caravan park. Despite his protestations – 'I'm not mental' – Boogers was sent out on loan – and subsequent free transfer – to Groningen.

2. **Claudio Taffarel**

The World Cup-winning goalkeeper and penalty shoot-out hero from USA 94 decided to hang up his gloves after suffering a breakdown – of the mechanical kind. The 37-year-old Brazilian encountered problems with his car as he drove from Parma to Empoli, where he was due to sign a contract. He took the roadside difficulties with his BMW as a 'sign' that he shouldn't prolong his football career and issued a statement to supporters of Empoli. 'I want to apologise to the club and to the fans, but this little inconvenience made me think about things a lot,' he said. 'I just felt I was doing something that wasn't going to please me, and that fate was sending me a message that for me football was finished. My goal now is to stay in Italy and open a restaurant in Parma.'

3. **Carlos Roa**

The Argentinian goalkeeper suffered from PMT – pre-millennial tension – a stress that afflicted a number of people in the run-up to the year 2000. Many normally rational individuals became convinced the world would come to an end at the turn of the millennium. Bearing in mind that Roa was a 'keeper, his mental state was probably fragile anyway, so perhaps it's not such a surprise that the man whose decisive penalty shoot-out save from David Batty sealed England's fate at World Cup '98 became a member of an 'apocalypse cult'. He refused to discuss a new contract with his team, Real Mallorca, because of it.

4. **Owen Hargreaves**

   He appears to be there, on the pitch, wearing an England shirt. But why? What does it mean?

5. **Faustino Asprilla and George Reynolds**

   A Tyneside legend, not least for an unforgettable hat-trick that beat Barcelona in St James' Park's first ever Champions League game, 'Tino' spent two years at Newcastle United between 1996/98. Then, following spells with Parma and Palmeiras, the Columbian nearly returned to the north-east. To play for *Darlington*. Asprilla agreed a deal with chairman George Reynolds, only to have a 5 a.m. panic attack and leg-it onto a flight to Colombia. Reynolds was not having that, and so conducted a legendary local radio interview from the pitch in which he pretended to be both the player as well as himself, turning in a classic 'Julio Geordio' performance.

6. **Carl Richards**

   Striker Richards had a blazing row with Blackpool caretaker manager Tommy White (brother of the late John White of the double-winning Spurs team, incidentally, who died in 1964 after being struck by lightning while playing golf) in a match against Chester in 1989. It was half-time and the argument ended with Richards taking off his boots and chucking them in the showers. Those were the days of only one substitute, so Richards' attitude problem did nothing to improve the situation for Blackpool as they only had a defender on the bench. They ended up losing 3–1 (although, technically speaking, they were already relegated anyway, as usual). Richards never played for them again.

7. **Augustin 'Tin Man' Delgado**

The striker signed in 2001 for Southampton from Necaxa was one of those cases who appears to have Munchausen's Syndrome by Proxy. He was the especially irritating sort of malingerer who, though he spent most of his time in the club treatment room, could always make a miracle recovery in order to find his way out of the country to get a game for his national side. With a record of 11 appearances in 3 seasons, for 0 goals, the Ecuadorian once prompted manager Gordon Strachan to say that he 'had a yogurt to eat that was more important than Delgado'. The Saints finally loaned him back to an Ecuadorian club and then cancelled his contract. Southampton fans took the view that the £3.5 million their team invested in the 'Tin Man' might have been better spent on a Bin Man.

7 TRIUMPHS OVER ADVERSITY

1. **Asa Hartford**

In the early '70s the young Scottish midfielder was about to transfer from West Brom to Leeds when routine tests revealed that he had a hole-in-the-heart condition. Leeds pulled out of the deal, but after treatment Asa defied the medical condition that would have ended many careers. Manchester City signed him for £210,000 in 1974. In a career that also took in spells at Forest, Everton and Norwich he went on to play in about 500 more competitive matches, and is in the top 20 of the elite group of players who have completed 700 or more English League games. An industrious and inventive midfielder, he scored his fair share of goals and was famous for his tenacious tackle. Hartford won 50 full caps and led Scotland to the 1982 World Cup Finals. Hartford was the subject of one of commentator David Coleman's most classic 'Colemanballs' when he described him as a 'whole-hearted player'.

2. **Djibril Cissé**

Cissé suffered a horrific injury as he went down under an innocuous challenge from Blackburn defender, Jay McEveley, in a league match in 2004. The French striker appeared to catch his foot in the turf and his leg contorted into a sickening shape as he fell to the ground. Cissé suffered a comminuted fracture of the tibia and a fracture of the fibula; 'comminuted' is a diagnosis which usually implies that the bone has been broken into more than two pieces. He later revealed that had it not been for prompt attention from the trainers at the stadium (who had to pull his bones back into place with their hands), he would probably have lost the leg below the knee. He had pins inserted, and was expected to be out of action for the rest of the 2004/05 season, but in fact recovered well enough to play in Liverpool's extraordinary Champions League final triumph over AC Milan in the same campaign, coming on as a sub for Milan Baros and scoring in the penalty shoot-out.

3. **Stig Tøfting**

When he was 13, the Danish player who turned out for Bolton Wanderers in the 2002/03 season found his parents dead at home after an apparent murder-suicide.

To make it as a professional footballer *at all* is some

achievement in the light of that background, but it's hardly the end of Tøfting's story. He appears to have been born under the wrong star: his tiny son died from meningitis in 2003. Tøfting carried the body of the 22-day-old boy in a white casket into church at a private funeral in his hometown of Aarhus, in Denmark, then spent some time with his family before going off to serve a four-month prison sentence for assault, a conviction handed down as a consequence of an incident in a restaurant after a World Cup night out with Danish team-mates. After he had served his time, he signed with AGF Aarhus in 2004, but was quickly released after a fight during a Christmas party.

4. **Gary Mabbutt**

Gary Mabbutt began his career at Bristol Rovers. No one could decide his best position, the team played in the drab surroundings of Eastville Stadium, and before he had reached the age of 18 it was discovered he was diabetic. Mabbutt did not allow the diagnosis to prevent him from enjoying a brilliant career – he went on to make over 600 appearances for Tottenham Hotspur, and to win 16 England caps. He famously appeared on the BBC children's television program Blue Peter where he demonstrated injecting insulin into an orange to show how he dealt with his condition on a daily basis. With Spurs he won the UEFA Cup in 1984, and captained the club to victory in the 1991 FA Cup Final.

5. **Alan Stubbs**

The former Celtic defender has fought testicular cancer twice after it returned following initial treatment in 2001. Stubbs marked his comeback the second time with a goal against Hibernian at Easter Road, and went on to play 142 games for Everton before moving on to Sunderland in 2005.

6. Markus Babbel

The German international who signed for Liverpool from Bayern Munich was a virtual ever-present in Liverpool's historic treble Cup-winning side of the 2000/01 season (the treble of the League, FA, and UEFA Cup – no other British side has reached three major cup finals in one season, let alone won them all). But soon after this Babbel fell prey to an illness that caused him to lose weight, making it difficult for him to train. It was found he had contracted Guillain-Barre Syndrome, an inflammation of the nervous system, and at one point it was reported that he was close to death. His recuperation involved a loan spell at Blackburn Rovers before the defender returned to Germany with VfB Stuttgart in 2004.

7. Bert Trautmann

The man himself. Trautmann was enlisted into the Wehrmacht at the outbreak of the Second World War, and by 1945 he had been court martialled for sabotage (he was a paratrooper), captured by the Russians and escaped; captured by the Free French and escaped; captured by the Americans and escaped before finally being captured by the British, who, so the tale has it, greeted him with the immortal line, 'Hello Fritz, fancy a cup of tea?' He ended up in a POW Camp at Ashton-in-Makerfield where he saw out the last days of the war and enjoyed the odd football match. Originally a centre forward, Trautmann went in goal when injury prevented him from competing outfield. His natural talent was recognised and he was scouted by St Helen's Town, where he first attracted the attentions of Manchester City. He moved to City in 1949 but was not exactly an instant crowd favourite: there was outrage from City fans, as well as from beyond, regarding the signing of a German player. There were threats of boycotts and letters of disapproval, but Bert overcame these odds to become an immortal at the Maine Road club, and to earn the respect of the whole football community. He made 545 appearances in total for the Blues, but his legend was sealed during the 1956 FA Cup Final. In the 75th minute with City leading 3–1, Trautmann dived at a ball and was temporarily knocked out in a head-collision with an oncoming Birmingham attacker. He continued to play for the remaining 15 minutes (at the time there were no substitutes). Manchester City held on for the victory, with Trautmann the hero due to his spectacular saves in the last minutes of the match. Three days later, an X-ray revealed he had broken a vertebra in his neck during the collision: he had effectively played out the game with a broken neck. In 2004 he was awarded an Honorary OBE.

MARCHING OFF TO WAR – THE 10 CLUBS THAT SENT MOST MEN TO SERVICE IN WORLD WAR II

1.	Crystal Palace	98
2.	Wolves	91
3.	Liverpool	76
4.	Chester	69 *
5.	Luton	68
6.	Huddersfield	65
7.	Leicester	63
8.	Charlton	62
9.	Oldham	60
10.	Grimsby	58

Two of these became Bevin Boys. A Bevin Boy was a young British man conscripted to work in the coal mines of the United Kingdom, from December 1943 until the end of World War II. Chosen at random from among the conscripts, nearly 48,000 Bevin Boys performed vital but largely unrecognised service in the coal mines, many not being released until years after the war. 10 per cent of all conscripts aged 18–25 were picked for this service.

(Source: Jack Rollin, Soccer at War 1939–45, *Headline Book Publishing Ltd, 2005.)*

LANGUAGE
EL LINGO

WHEN I MET HARRY
By **Stephen Foster**

A DOZEN HARRY REDKNAPPS
LOST IN TRANSLATION
SHALL WE SING A SONG FOR YOU?
ALLITERATIVE XI
10 PLAYERS WITH ONLY ONE 4-LETTERED NAME
10 OF STUART BUTLER'S EXCELLENT FOOTBALL HAIKUS
15 MOMENTS OF COMMENTARY
10 OLD NICKNAMES
5 ROBINS

WHEN I MET HARRY

Stephen Foster tries to persuade **Harry Redknapp** that he's come out with a few good lines

I live 200 miles away from where I was born, so I travel a lot to see my team play (sharp-eyed persons may have noted the bias of information about a particular Midlands side in this book). Because I travel a lot, I listen to sports radio a lot. After the match I drive slowly from the ground in order to remain in the local radio reception area long enough to hear the post-match interview with the manager, even though for the last few seasons this has been a pointless exercise, because the boss gave the same spiel week after week no matter what the outcome of the game: 'The lads are an honest bunch, work hard, we just need that extra bit of quality up front, Nigel.' After satisfying myself that it was situation normal on the honesty, hard work and absence of quality up-front scene, I put my foot down.

Re-tuned to national radio, it's pretty much more of the same – a parade of New Labour gaffers, media-trained by Politburo Central, all droning on about attitude and application.

But once in a while, if you're lucky, you pick up a gem like this: 'I told my chairman that David O'Leary spent £18 million to buy Rio Ferdinand from us and Leeds had given O'Leary £5.5 million in share options, whereas I bring in £18 million and all I get is a bacon sandwich.'

Nine times out of ten, the outstanding comment comes from Harry Redknapp.

And so it is that I find myself waiting in the foyer of a country-style hotel in Suffolk (the type of place where football teams hang out before away matches) one midweek afternoon, intending to speak to Harry about his place in the lexicon of football. He emerges into the wood-panelled lobby wearing a club sweatshirt, club shorts, socks of the kind you wear with a suit, no further footwear, and a bemused expression. Something has been lost in the wash between me, his secretary at Southampton and himself, and throughout our conversation he's never quite sure what I'm trying to find out. When I put it to him that he has a particular and colourful way with language, an arresting figure of speech, and it is *this* that I'm hoping to talk about, he laughs in a perplexed manner, as if I might be making it up, and takes a half-glance round the otherwise deserted lobby to see if he can spot the hidden camera.

Still, he gives me the benefit of the doubt, and we settle into a couple of sofas. I have a rough list of questions: who are the great talkers of the game, the ones he admires? Which managers left an impression when he was a player? What are his preferred methods in the team talk? And so on. All this is greeted by a shake of the head and further bemusement. So I try another: any early influences?

The answer to this is a half-hour anecdote about the boys in his class, the ones who left school without even being able to read or write (not him), about routine bobbing-off, hanging with the naughty kids, smoking (not him) in the bogs, that he worked hard when he was little, that his family were dockers and cleaners, grafters; that he went 'oppin' (hop picking in

177

Kent) with his Nan in the closed season when he first started out at West Ham United, an activity of his that manager Ron Greenwood ('old-school, talked a bit posh') could never understand. 'We were supposed to paint the ground up during the summer, the crush barriers and all that,' he says (can't you just picture Rio Ferdinand up a ladder?), 'But I said to Ron Greenwood that I couldn't do that, 'cos I was off 'oppin' with me Nan. He never understood – "'oppin', what's 'oppin'?" – he'd go. Any event, next time he'd clap eyes on me it'd be for pre-season training.' He doesn't laugh at this, he shakes his head at the gap of comprehension between a person who didn't understand 'oppin' and himself. His picture of this world is neatly adumbrated – working with working people was one part of his life, but football was always the principal passion and the way up to better things and good money.

Having listened to all this, I attempt to get the thing back on track: I make further efforts to persuade him that he is in any sense quote-worthy (he chuckles as I read a couple of his best lines back to him, as if somebody else probably said them), and so our conversation turns to other talkers. Ron Atkinson's name comes up.

'Good bloke, I tell you what though,' he says, 'He made a proper ricket, didn't he, and it's cost him dear.'

He is alluding to the comment Atkinson made 'off mic' when he referred to the Chelsea defender Marcel Desailly in racist terms at the end of a game in Monaco. While Redknapp rehearses the defence of Atkinson that was tried out at the time – that he signed a lot of black players – he absolutely agrees that the word he used (the 'n' word) is unacceptable.

'You wouldn't have said that?' I say.

'Oh no,' he replies. 'I'd have just called him a lazy bastard.'

Harry has to go – he has a team to prepare. He sorts me out a nice comp. for the game (the Saints are playing at Ipswich in a few hours' time), and wanders off. I hope he never reads this, and gets any ideas about himself, because it strikes me that it's the absence of any notion that he has a gift with the lingo that makes him so good at it; the last thing you'd want would be anyone coaching it out of him.

A DOZEN
HARRY REDKNAPPS

Harry Redknapp, Valentine's day, 1972

1. HIS Christian name was at least appropriate, given that his performances for us were worth about two-bob.

On Romanian Florin Raducioiu, for whom he paid £1.5 million in 1996.

2. It was amazing, given the ferocity of his tackles and his near-obsessive hatred of training, that he wasn't always injured. In fact I don't think I ever saw him do a stretching exercise, and he couldn't touch his toes if you gave him 10 grand.
On Julian Dicks.

3. Even when they had Moore, Hurst and Peters, West Ham's average finish was about 17th. It just shows how crap the other 8 of us were.
On his playing heyday.

4. With the foreign players it's more difficult. Most of them don't even bother with the golf, they don't want to go racing. They don't even drink.
On la cultural différence.

5. Dani is so good-looking I don't know whether to play him or f*ck him.
On the Portuguese playboy loanee from Sporting Lisbon. Dani was never made a permanent signing on account of excessive nightclubbing and stuff.

6. Hartson's got more previous than Jack the Ripper.
On the disciplinary record of the striker who famously aimed a kick at the head of teammate Eyal Berkovic in training.

7. I tape over most of them with *Corrie* or *Neighbours*. Most of them are crap. They can f***ing make anyone look good. I signed Marco Boogers off a video. He was a good player but a nutter. They didn't show that on the video.
On what he does with the videos he is sent promoting players. Although he still signs them up of course.

8. I left a couple of my foreigners out last week and they started talking in 'foreign'. I knew what they were saying: 'Blah, blah, blah, le b****** manager, f****** useless b******!'

   On his original days at Portsmouth.

9. To be honest, even the dinner lady didn't want to see him again.

   On the return of Julian Dicks from his spell with Liverpool.

10. He's got a broken tie-up.

    On the injury-prone Robbie Slater.

11. Samassi Abou don't speak the English too good.

    Self-explanatory.

12. The lad went home to the Ivory Coast and got a bit of food poisoning. He must have eaten a dodgy missionary or something.

    More trouble for Samassi.

LOST IN TRANSLATION

With opportunities for travel and overseas employment, players need to be more multi-lingual than a multi-lingual secretary these days.

1. *Ninety-five per cent of my language problems are the fault of that stupid little midget.*

   Gianfranco Zola remembers former Chelsea team-mate **Dennis Wise** (and coming from one so vertically challenged, note the world class insult-within-an-insult here).

2. *Q. Do you speak good Russian?*
   A. I know the dirty words.

   José Mourinho explains how he communicates with Roman Abramovich.

3. *Hijo de puta!*

   David Beckham gets himself sent off in his last league game of the 2004 season for calling the referee the 'son of a whore'. The dirty words are always the easiest to pick up.

4. *At last England have appointed a manager who speaks English better than the players.*

   Brian Clough on **Sven-Göran Eriksson**

5. *Only if we realise how sh*t we were at Blackburn can we improve.*

   Paolo Di Canio demonstrating an easy grasp of the vernacular, offers an assessment of Sheffield Wednesday.

6. *You can't say my team aren't winners. They've proved that by finishing fourth, third and second in the last three years.*

   Gérard Houllier, Liverpool manager

7. *I can understand everyone, everyone except Ray Parlour.*

   Junichi Inamoto of Arsenal and Japan, struggling to tune his ear to the demotic of the 'Romford Pele'.

8. *That's rubbish. There are three things in life where you do not need a common language – football, music and sex.*

   Turkey's **Rustu Recber**, on learning that he wouldn't be picked by Barcelona until he learns Spanish.

9. *I sweated and sweated to get there [Wembley] more than any*

man should have to. *I've been given the elbow so many times since starting my first job coaching the amateurs Sheffield FC. Since then I've run myself into the ground, trying to prove that even if you speak funny you can have talent.*

Danny Bergara, Stockport's Uruguayan manager in 1992.

10. *'I wonder why in the English language it's called the Czech Republic when they have a name of their own – Czechi. That's one for the pedagogues out there among the football-watching public.'*

'So are we calling them Czechi now George??'

George Hamilton terrifies his co-pundit **Ray Houghton** on RTE.

SHALL WE SING A SONG FOR YOU?

If you're talking jazz, then improvisation has a bad name, but it can raise a smile in even the most difficult circumstances when a set of fans get it right.

1. *Scoreboard, scoreboard, what's the score?*
   Sung by Blackpool fans at Bournemouth when the scoreboard got stuck as Blackpool started winning. Yes, that's what it says: Blackpool started winning.

2. *Down with the soufflé, you're going down with the soufflé.*
   Chelsea fans cook with gas as their team send Norwich City to the bottom of the Premiership. Celebrity chef Delia Smith is Norwich City's principal investor.

3. *Are you here to roll the pitch?*
   Stoke City followers exhibit their legendary wit as they make an enquiry of a particularly rotund groundsman at half-time at Colchester United.

4. *Oh lucky lucky, lucky lucky lucky lucky Liverpool.*
   Crystal Palace fans keep a fine sense of perspective after their 9–0 defeat at Anfield in 1989.

5. *We all came in the same taxi, same taxi, same taxi.*
   The Wimbledon choir comment on the size of their own support.

6. *City of culture, you're having a laugh, City of culture, you're having a laugh.*
   Manchester United fans find it hard to believe that Liverpool will be the European Centre of Excellence in the Arts in 2008.

7. *You've got Di Canio, We've got your stereos.*
   As if to emphasise the validity of the United fans' point, the Kop respond to West Ham's, *Paolo Di Canio, Paolo Di Canio!* (According to legend, Hammers fans were the first to adapt 'La Donna e Mobile' from *Rigoletto* by Giuseppe Verdi as a football chant, for Di-Can-io.)

8. *One Harry Potter, there's only one Harry Potter.*
   Grimsby followers demonstrate the art of making your own amusement as they harass a bespectacled young steward at Stockport, incessantly, all game long.

9. *Stayed in the kitchen, you should have stayed in the kitchen.*

Bristol City fans come over all sympathetic when lineswoman Wendy Toms has to go off injured during a game at Ashton Gate.

10. *Have you ever seen your dick?*

The Millwall support question a roly-poly West Ham fan as he emerges from an executive box to 'give it large'.

11. *Two Andy Gorams, there's only two Andy Gorams.*

Celtic fans taunt Rangers' goalkeeper Andy Goram amid rumours that he's suffering from schizophrenia.

12. *One team in Tallinn; there's only one team in Tallinn.*

A World Cup qualifier beween Estonia and Scotland in 1996: in preparation for the 6.45 p.m. kick-off Estonian officials had arranged temporary floodlighting from Finland. Scotland complained to FIFA that this would cause problems for the goalkeepers. The next morning, to rectify the problem, FIFA announced the game would kick off at 3 p.m. and not 6.45 p.m. Scotland were able to 'rally the troops' in time, but Estonian officials complained that other matters made this awkward – security arrangements for the stadium, consideration of supporters working through the day – and that some players were 80 km from the ground. The most important thing, however, was that the television contract for coverage was arranged for a 6.45 p.m. kick-off. Just before three o'clock John Collins led Scotland out as the only team on the pitch. It was at this point that Scotland supporters sang their song.

The game kicked off: Billy Dodds tapped the ball to Collins. The ref blew his whistle for the second time in two seconds and the match was over. Scotland were awarded a 3–0 default win. The ball was booted towards the support, whereby one large kilted fan burst through the 'security cordon' and delicately flicked the match ball onto the pitch. He ran on unchallenged towards the empty Estonian net, carefully managing not to spill any of his beer on the way, and with theatrical nonchalance hammered the ball past the non-existent 'keeper. Good lad.

12. *Bob the Builder*

QPR fans started singing the 2000 Christmas number one during a fixture between Bournemouth and QPR after the Tannoy announcer had asked for an electrician to report to reception, and then one minute later requested a plumber.

13. *Two nil or not two nil?*

Leamington fans contemplating the slings and arrows of outrageous fortune as their team go 2–0 ahead against Stratford Town away.

ALLITERATIVE XI

Carlo Cudicini

Bobby Balde   Didier Deschamps   Nacho Novo   Malky Mackay

Kevin Keegan   Zinedine Zidane   Billy Bremner

Ade Akinbiyi   Dixie Dean   Jermaine Jenas

10 PLAYERS WITH ONLY ONE 4-LETTERED NAME

1. **Pele**
2. **Deco**
3. **Xavi**
4. **Dani**
5. **Cafu**
6. **Didi**
7. **Kaka**
8. **Alex**
9. **Zico**
10. **Mido**

and a special mention for:

11. all those players known to fans as **'Shit'**

10 OF STUART BUTLER'S EXCELLENT FOOTBALL HAIKUS

A traditional Japanese form, the haiku is a seventeen-syllable poem consisting of three units of five, seven and five syllables. Like 4–4–2, or even 3–5–2, it's a poetic form that understands the importance of keeping its shape.

1. **Changed my Mind about Brazil**
   When I watch Brazil,
   It's just like watching Brazil.
   Do I not like that.

2. The Old Man(ager) on the Moon

On a bench in Space,
The Manager on the Moon.
Still not over it.

3. Cup Final Punditry and Ecology

The globe spins in space.
Like a football, it will burst
With too much hot air.

4. Football as a state of alienated Love

Trish is all I wish;
She is my satellite dish,
Sky, sun, moon and stars.

5. From John Ball to Football and Bad Language

We swore sacred oaths,
Until base profanity
Brought foul victory.

6. Why a Football is Round

The ball is a sphere,
Because if it was oblong,
It would hurt your ear.

7. Football Sums

Football unites us,
But racism divides us,
Unity adds up.

8. Copse and Robbers

Leaves come tumbling down;
More falling with each new day:
Like attendances.

It's (roughly) this shape for a reason (otherwise it would hurt your ear).One of the two balls used in the first 1930 World Cup final between Argentina and Uruguay: the teams could not agree on which ball to use, so they decided to use an Argentinian ball in the first half and a Uruguayan ball (as pictured) in the second half.

9. **Philosophical Doubt Removed**
   When I watch Brazil,
   It's just like watching Brazil.
   Life's like that sometimes.

10. **Association Football** *
    HQ finds guilt by
    Association. Football
    Says Peace is the goal.

(* On Christmas Day 1914, during World War I, a Scotland vs Germany friendly football match broke out in No Man's Land. It finished 3–2 in favour of Fritz.)

15 MOMENTS OF COMMENTARY

Close your ears if you're of a sensitive disposition. Some of the logic here is more tortured than the soul of Eric Cantona.

1. Real Madrid are like a rabbit in the glare of the headlights in the face of Manchester United's attacks. But this rabbit comes with a suit of armour in the shape of two precious away goals.
   George Hamilton, *RTE*

2. More football in a moment – but first, highlights of the Scottish League Cup Final.
   Gary Newbon, *ITV*

3. Merseyside derbies usually last 90 minutes, and I'm sure today's won't be any different.
   Sir Trevor Brooking, *BBC*

4. Don't tell those coming in now the result of that fantastic match. Now let's have another look at Italy's winning goal.
   David Coleman, *BBC*

5. They have won sixty-six games, and they've scored in all of them.
   Brian Moore, *ITV (on Rosenborg)*

6. Gary Lineker has now scored 37 goals. That is precisely twice as many as last year.
   John Motson, *BBC*

7. And now for the goals at Carrow Road where it ended nil–nil.
   Elton Welsby, *ITV*

8. There are two ways of getting the ball. One is from your own teammates, and that's the only way.
   Terry Venables, *ITV*

9. Some of Paul Scholes' tackles come in so late they arrive yesterday.
   Clive Tyldesley, *ITV*

10. What will you do when you leave football, Jack – will you stay in football?
    Stuart Hall, *BBC*

11. Well, either side could win it, or it could be a draw.
    Ron Atkinson, *ITV*

12. If Bill Shankly was alive, he'd be turning in his grave.
    Harry, a caller to the BBC's 606 phone-in programme, after Liverpool's Cup defeat by Burnley.

13. And they'll be dancing in the streets of Total Network Solutions tonight.
*Sky's **Jeff Stelling** as TNS capture the Welsh title*

14. Defenders often fall into the mistake of marking space – they see all that space and they mark it. But space doesn't score the goal: it's the player that does that!
*West Bromwich Albion striker **Kevin Campbell** gives 'expert summary' on BBC Radio Five*

And finally, back to the master for one more:

15. When I said they'd scored two goals, of course I meant they'd scored one.
*Of course you did, George. **George Hamilton** of RTE*

10 OLD NICKNAMES

1.	Barnsley	Colliers (now Tykes)
2.	Brighton	Shrimps (now Seagulls)
3.	Coventry	Bantams (now Sky Blues – even worse)
4.	Everton	The Black Watch – briefly* (now Toffees)
5.	Lincoln City	Citizens or Cits or even Window Blinds for their red and white stripes (now Red Imps)
5.	Luton	Strawplaiters (now Hatters)
6.	Middlesbrough	Ironsides (now Boro – very imaginative)
7.	Notts County	Lambs (now Magpies)

8.	Palace	Glaziers (now Eagles – it was Malcolm Allison who made the change to this daft name)
9.	Reading	Biscuitmen (now Royals)
10.	Sunderland	Rokerites (now Black Cats)

* In 1879, before football was a properly organised sport, a player recruited from another team could still turn out wearing the jersey of his former club, which led to much confusion. It was under these conditions that Everton decided on a unified kit and so, to avoid purchasing a brand new one, they dyed all the various shirts of their players black. A two-inch wide scarlet sash was added and the Merseysiders adopted the nickname The Black Watch after the famous military regiment.

5 ROBINS

The Robins is the most common nickname. It is used by:

1. Bristol City
2. Cheltenham
3. Charlton
4. Swindon
5. Wrexham

HUMAN
SOCIETY AND
INSTITUTIONS
THE EXECUTIVE SUITE

LOVE THY NEIGHBOUR
By **Magnus Eriksson**

STUART COSGROVE'S 10 REASONS WHY
ST JOHNSTONE FC ARE THE COOLEST
FOOTBALL TEAM IN THE WORLD

SUBBUTEO – 11 FLICK-TO-KICK FACTS

FIRMS – 11 HOOLIGAN GROUPS
AND THEIR DAFT NAMES

THE 6 CONFEDERATIONS OF FIFA

FC ALCATRAZ

WHY DID THE CHICKEN CROSS THE ROAD?

LOVE THY NEIGHBOUR

Swedish journalist **Magnus Eriksson** outlines who hates who on the Scandinavian scene (and why this means he sometimes ends up supporting Germany).

The Greek-Swedish writer Theodor Kallifatides once stated that a man can leave his country, he can abandon his family and friends, as well as his politics and faith, but he can never abandon his team. Kallifatides' team is Panathinaikos from Athens. In general Swedes tend to support our nation's eleven, the local team, and an English one. Sometimes we even support a Scottish team, at least when Henrik Larsson plays for Celtic.

There are, however, some exceptions. In Scania, the most southern province of Sweden, we long ago embraced the Danish eleven as our own team. When the Danish beat England at Wembley in the European Cup qualifiers in 1983 and thus made it to the final round the year after, most other Swedes did the same, even labelling the Danes the Brazilians of the North. Needless to say, at that time the Swedish team was not performing very well.

Apart from embracing the Danish, most Scandinavians tend to agree on which teams to detest, in general, and which teams to detest in particular. We abhor our neighbours (except the Danes). Like most of the world, we hate the Germans even more. And like everyone, at least outside Great Britain and Spain, we love Brazil.

But of course our love and hate stories reflect quite a bit of life's not always so charming inconsistencies. In the '90s, many Swedes considered Norway's national team the most boring in the world. After all, it was led by an old Mao Zedong supporter, and it seemed to play the game according to some Marxist–Leninist tactics. But we had a hard time detecting the obvious; that if Norway was the world's most boring team, then Sweden was the self-evident runner-up for the title.

The attitude towards Germany is another paradox. Everyone wants attacking football. We might admire the Italians for their brilliance and tactical skills, but we also find them unbelievably dull – after all, their main reason for being seems to be to defend their own goal. Yet everyone, or next to everyone, hates the Germans in spite of their playing the world's most relentlessly attacking game (at least since the English learned to defend themselves, from the Gospel according to Sven-Göran). How can this be?

I guess that the dislike of German football could be interpreted from a post-colonial point of view, although we'd have to change perspective completely. We have an idealised model, not of Western rationality but of Brazilian excellence. For some reason we find the Germans, more than most teams (except Scotland), at fault in this model. While the colonial 'other', the native, was an incarnation of everything opposite to Western rationality, German football is regarded as a mean machine: tactics-bound, un-improvisational, stereotypical, sterile, always the hit-and-run. The idealised Brazilian model, on the other hand, represents all the good, even morally good features: playful, technical, improvisational, almost erotic. That is a process of 'otherising' as good as any.

The Swedish love-story with Brazilian football has a significant origin. The 1958 World Cup was played in Sweden. For the first time Sweden used professional players who had returned home from their international clubs. But only those who had returned: that is why the late, great Gunnar Nordahl, the record goal-scorer in the Italian league, did not play the tournament. One of his friends, Nils Liedholm (in the '80s, the successful coach of Roma), scored the first goal in the final. Yes, we made it to the finals. Yes, we made the first goal. And yes, Brazil finally beat us 5–2.

That was Brazil's first world championship. Elderly Swedes speak fondly of the impression the Brazilians made when they watched them in the arenas – or on TV. The tournament didn't just mark the breakthrough of national Swedish television, but also of a young genius, Pele. The tournament is definitely Swedish football history, but also the stuff that Brazilian legends are made of. Some Swedes believe that the Brazilians' yellow shirt is a homage to us. Although not true, it is the stuff that love is made of. And dreams.

But the Swedish love for Brazilian football can be tiresome. Even when Brazil is beaten they are considered the world's best team. The technically brilliant Turkish players were reduced to just being 'capable' by Swedish commentators in the game against Brazil in the first round of the 2002 World Cup. When Denilson did his ludicrous *Riverdance* act around the ball in the 1998 World Cup, he was hailed for his technical excellence. Never mind that he delayed the team's offensive attack. That is why I cherish the memory of Thuram vs Denilson in the final that year. Thuram just sighed when watching Denilson jumping like a frog around the ball. He sighed, snatched the ball, and ran. It reminded me somehow of Indiana Jones sighing at the Egyptian sword master's show-off before shooting him. And we still believe that the otherwise unquestionably great Ronaldinho showed magnificent skill when he placed his fluke free-kick behind David Seaman, because although we love English football up here in the Arctic, there is one thing we love even more: Brazilian football. Never mind the inconsistency of that kind of love. The ideal result between Sweden and England seems to be a draw, while it is okay to get beaten by Brazil. We are not always so patriotic. As long as we defeat our neighbours, the larger football nations may very well have a go at us. But there is one exception – Germany. And maybe Italy, at least since they so totally failed to realise the irony of the 2–2 draw between Denmark and Sweden in the first round of the 2004 European Cup. It was not intentional, but we thought it very funny. The Italians did not, since that was exactly the result that would send them home.

That is the view from Stockholm. Not all agree, however I tend to become more and more sympathetic to Krautball. And I like the Scots as well.

STUART
COSGROVE'S
10 REASONS WHY ST JOHNSTONE FC ARE THE COOLEST FOOTBALL TEAM IN THE WORLD

**Never won the
Forfarshire Cup**

1. THEY are the only team in Britain with a 'J' in their name. Lesser teams like Juventus of Italy can make similar claims, but they have never won the Forfarshire Cup.

2. St Johnstone were the first team in Scotland with a purpose-built all-seater stadium.

3. Saints are the only team in the UK whose record crowd was not at a football match but at a congregational meeting held by the American evangelical preacher Billy Graham.

4. At St Johnstone's old ground, Muirton Park, the top scorer in a single game was not a footballer. The famous basketball player Meadowlark Lemon of the Harlem Globetrotters racked up the record tally in an exhibition game against a team of red Indians.

5. St Johnstone are the only British team to put three goals past Fabien Barthez whilst his girlfriend was watching. Supermodel Linda Evangelista watched Saints put three past her bald beau in the home leg of a UEFA Cup match against AS Monaco.

6. Celebrity fans are us. St Johnstone can lay claim to Ewan McGregor but he is only a B-list tease. Pontius Pilate, the Roman Governor who crucified Jesus Christ, was born in a Roman encampment at Fortingall, near Perth. His father was a legionnaire stationed in the village. So Pontius Pilate's local team was St Johnstone.

7. Although Queen of the South are the only British team whose name appears in the Bible, St John the Baptist, the patron saint of Perth, appears much more often. It is St John's Town that gives the club its name.

8. St Johnstone's 1971 team famously beat SV Hamburg, Rangers, Celtic and Charlton all in the same season, but alas, they were narrowly beaten by Real Madrid in the Bernabeu, who had taken a shock lead.

9. The club's most famous striker, Henry Hall, was named after a famous pre-war bandleader. The original Henry Hall conducted the house orchestra at Gleneagles Hotel near Perth, and appeared in the first outside broadcast concert transmitted by the BBC. His namesake, the real Henry Hall, was a balding gym teacher, who scored goals for fun in the '70s.

10. Unlike Manchester United, Chelsea, AC Milan and Ajax, St Johnstone FC have won the Scottish First Division Championship three times, a feat that no Brazilian team has ever achieved. But unlike Fife rivals Raith Rovers, St Johnstone have never been shipwrecked on their way to a pre-season friendly.

SUBBUTEO – 11 FLICK-TO-KICK FACTS

1. Named after the Latin word for hobby, Subbuteo is sold in over 50 countries.

2. The estimated number of figures manufactured since Subbuteo began is 500 million and rising.

3. The world record for playing Subbuteo is 62 hours and 7 minutes. It was set in 1986 by Tim Peters and Paul Chambers.

4. Over 700 different kits have appeared on the figures.

5. In 1992 a brave but fruitless attempt was made to have Subbuteo made an Olympic sport.

6. The creator of Subbuteo, Peter Adolph, was a Queens Park Rangers fan. When he died in 1994 his coffin was adorned with a 3ft Subbuteo figure in a QPR strip.

7. A special non-football edition was made for about two years in 1964/65 which contained the four Beatles either playing the drums or playing a guitar. To what end, who can say? (Though quite often 5-a-side teams *do* go a man down.) There was also a *Space Planet* Subbuteo.

8. Royal Doulton produce a limited edition of 5-inch-tall ceramic Subbuteo players. Don't even think about flick-to-kicking these in a Boys vs Girls Little Bo Peep-sponsored tournament, not if you want to live, says Auntie Violet.

9. Subbuteo streaker: Tom Taylor, who owns a shop in mid-Wales and has sold 6000 sets of Subbuteo, began to sell hand-painted streakers after seeing one at a real match in 1998. Available in male or female ('They've got all the bits. To me it's not offensive, we're all like that underneath, though you may need to buy a magnifying glass', said Tom), the streakers are also sold in a special-edition set with a chasing policeman and a helmet to cover the offending area.

You may need a magnifying glass

10. Three black players were added to the England team in 1987 to (rather belatedly) take account of real life (nine years earlier in 1978, Viv Anderson made his debut as the first black England player, in a 1–0 win against Czechoslovakia.)

11. In 1991 Half Man Half Biscuit recorded the classic song, 'All I want for Christmas is a Dukla Prague Away Kit'. Sample lyrics:

> *So he'd send his doting mother up the stairs*
> *To get Subbuteo out of the loft*
> *He had all the accessories required for that big*
>   *match atmosphere*
> *The crowd and the dugout and the floodlights too*
> *You'd always get palmed off with a headless centre*
>   *forward*
> *And a goalkeeper with no arms and a face like his*
> *And he'd managed to get hold of a Dukla Prague*
>   *away kit*
> *'Cos his uncle owned a sports shop and he'd kept it*
>   *to one side.*

FIRMS – 11 HOOLIGAN GROUPS AND THEIR DAFT NAMES

1. *Chelsea*: Headhunters (the elite Personnel Recruitment Company)

2. *Chesterfield*: Chesterfield Bastard Squad (Queen's Award for Plain English)

3. *Derby County*: Derby Lunatic Fringe (motto: Freedom for Tooting)

4. *Grimsby Town*: Cleethorpes Beach Patrol (dedicated to saving Harry the Haddock from drowning)

5. *Newcastle United*: The Gremlins (don't let them eat all the pies after midnight)

6. *Notts County*: Roadside Casuals (very casual, nobody bothers turning up)

7. *Portsmouth*: 6.57 (named after the departure time of their favourite train)

8. *Rochdale:* The Chosen Few (few being the *mot juste*)

9. *St Mirren*: Love Street Division (LSD – it was never a dive ref, it was a trip)

10. *Stoke City*: Naughty Forty (because they are so, er, naughty)

11. *Swansea City*: Swansea Jacks (named after a life-saving dog)

THE 6 CONFEDERATIONS OF FIFA

FIFA, the *Fédération International de Football Association*, is world football's governing body. FIFA has been dubbed the 'United Nations of Football', with 205 affiliated Associations. The Associated countries are governed by six Confederations, which support FIFA substantially in tasks such as the organisation of tournaments. The Confederations – the umbrella organisations of the national football associations on each continent – are:

1. Asian Football Confederation (AFC)

2. Confédération Africaine de Football (CAF)

3. Confederation of North, Central American and Caribbean Association Football (CONCACAF)

4. Confederación Sudamericana de Fútbol (CSF)

5. Oceania Football Confederation (OFC)

6. Union des Associations Européennes de Football (UEFA)

FC ALCATRAZ

The list of professional footballers and ex-pros who have form is as long as your arm; you could come up with enough old lags to start a tournament. Here is a select XI, chosen for the range and vision of their extra-curricular activity, and lining up in the hooky 4–4–1–1 system.

Safecracker hands

Peter Borota
The former Chelsea 'keeper was somehow managing to carve out a half-decent career as an artist until it was discovered that all the paintings he tried to pass off as his own were in fact stolen.

Backdoor four

Peter Storey (Captain)
Former Arsenal full-back Storey has been convicted of running a brothel called 'The Calypso Massage Parlour' in Leyton High Street, East London; plotting to counterfeit gold coins, stealing cars and importing pornographic videos in the spare wheel of his jeep. He was also given 28 days (suspended) in 1991 for swearing at a traffic warden.

Tony Adams

The Arsenal and England captain spent 56 days at Chelmsford Open Prison in 1990 after being convicted of drink-driving; Adams had previously been fined for driving in a drunken state several times. In September 1993 during a drinking bout he helped Ray Parlour spray Essex pizza-eaters with a fire extinguisher. He came out as an alcoholic in 1996 and subsequently set up a charity to help players deal with alcohol, drug and gambling addictions. Dangerously, he went on to live with Poppy Teacher, a member of the famous whisky family.

Andy Linighan

In 1993 the Arsenal centre-half was forced to apologise to Jewish taxi-driver Harold Levy for anti-Semitic remarks and refusing to pay a £63 metered fare from the PFA dinner at the Grosvenor House to his Harpenden home.

Jermaine Pennant

Pennant completes the all-Arsenal back door four. He once claimed he would have been as big as Wayne Rooney, had Arsenal boss Arsène Wenger shown a little more faith in him. He set about keeping himself at the forefront of Wenger's thoughts by getting himself nicked for drink-driving twice in a year, the second time diverting his Mercedes into a lamp-post at 6.20 a.m. He went down for a three-month loan spell at Her Majesty's Pleasure in 2005, and is deliberately being played out of position in this team to remind him not to be such a bad boy in future.

Midfield masterminds

Jamie Lawrence

Had a difficult boyhood in south London and ended up spending time in several young offenders' institutes before eventually finding himself sentenced to four years for robbery with violence. He was sent to serve his time on the Isle of Wight. On Boxing Day 1993, Lawrence played for the prison team against a semi-professional side, Cowes Sports, scoring twice. The Cowes manager asked the prison governor if Lawrence could play with them. He was released in 1993, and 90 days later he went on trial at Sunderland and impressed Terry Butcher sufficiently to earn himself a one-year deal. He signed on a Friday and made his debut as a substitute on the Sunday against Middlesbrough. The amusing PA man played 'Jailhouse Rock' as he warmed up. Lawrence went on to win 13 caps for Jamaica as well as a Littlewoods Cup medal with Leicester.

David Roche

Strongman midfielder who wasted his talent. Came through the ranks at Newcastle United and by all accounts could have been a brilliant player. But incidents off the pitch, including gang fights and late-night benders, ruined him. He moved down to Doncaster Rovers, then to Southend United, before finding himself involved in a serious shooting incident. He was eventually sentenced to eight years for involvement in a drug deal.

Nizar Trabelsi

Fortuna Düsseldorf in Germany thought they had found a promising striker when they signed Tunisian

Trabelsi in 1989. But they soon dropped him, and he drifted from team to team, developing a cocaine habit, and racking up criminal offences. Trabelsi confessed in a radio interview in 2001 to training with associates of Osama bin Laden in Afghanistan, and in 2003 he was sentenced to 10 years in prison for plotting to drive a car bomb into Kleine Brogel, a NATO airbase in Belgium where US military personnel work.

Mickey Thomas

We have already met Thomas in our **Naughty XI** (p.161) and now here he is again. He played for so many clubs, and picked up so many signing-on fees that his shopping habits must have surpassed Sir Elton John's: he appeared before the beak on charges of passing forged bank notes (twenties and tenners to trainees at Wrexham, during his club at the time) in 1993. His day in court began with him joking with reporters, 'Anyone got change of a tenner for the phone?' and finished up with an 18-month stretch.

In the hole

George Best

In addition to playing career that took in Manchester United, Stockport County, Cork Celtics, Los Angeles Aztecs, Fulham, Fort Lauderdale Strikers, Hibernian, San José Earthquakes, Bournemouth and Brisbane Lions, Best was to be found getting a game for the Ford Open Prison team for a while in 1982, after a small misunderstanding involving drink-driving, assaulting a policeman and jumping bail.

Doing solitary up front

Duncan Ferguson

Ferguson became the first British Footballer to serve a prison sentence as a result of an on-field incident when he headbutted Raith Rovers' John McStay during an SPL match in Scotland in 1994. He spent six weeks in the notorious Barlinnie prison, where violence and overcrowding were the norm, but Ferguson had played against Vinnie Jones, so he was used to that.

On the bench

Eric Cantona

Escaped jail but given community service, fined £20,000, and banned for nine months for the splendid kung-fu demonstration that put a Crystal Palace fan – who was hurling abuse at him at Selhurst Park in 1995 – back into his box.

John Burridge

Goalkeeping odd-ball 'Budgie' Burridge found himself on the wrong side of the law while manager of Blyth Spartans. The much-travelled 'keeper was convicted and fined for dealing in counterfeit leisure-wear, with the prosecution's case relying on video evidence of the Blyth players dressed in some of Budgie's 'hot' gear before a Cup game against Blackpool. Burridge pleaded poverty and went off to coach the national team of Oman.

Mr Big in the Dugout

Graham Rix

From an extensive list of applications the post has been

awarded to Gianluca Vialli's former assistant at Chelsea – later manager of Portsmouth, Oxford United and Heart of Midlothian. Rix was given 12 months in 1999 for having sex with a 15-year-old girl in a West London hotel on the eve of Chelsea's Premier League clash with Manchester United.

Mr Big in the Dugout's Right-Hand Man

Thomas Nkono

Cameroon's goalkeeping coach was arrested before his side's African Nations Cup semi-final against Mali by Malian policeman at pitchside in 2002. The coppers suspected Nkono of having thrown a gri-gri (a black magic charm) onto the playing field. The law and African football authorities agreed with them and banned the former Cameroonian international for a year.

WHY DID THE CHICKEN CROSS THE ROAD?

Some answers to the most popular online round-robin in football:

George Best

Because there was a bar on the other side?

David Beckham

Why would he be on a road? I thought chickens lived in the ocean.

Arsène Wenger

From my position in the dug-out I did not see the

incident clearly so I cannot really comment. However, I do think that he gets picked on by opposition players and fans who are clearly chicken-o-phobic.

Sir Alex Ferguson

As far as I'm concerned he crossed the road at least a minute early according to my watch.

José Mourinho

There is no pressure on the chicken: if the chicken thinks he is top one, then he can be top one, good, the pressure is all on the chickens behind him, the second and third chickens. The chicken is a special one, not one of the bottle.

Gianluca Vialli

When the fish are down, he'll just be one of the chaps. It doesn't matter to me whether he's an Italian, French or English chicken as long as he's willing to die on the pitch for the flock.

Glenn Hoddle

The chicken was hit by the lorry when crossing the road because in a previous life it had been a bad chicken.

Wayne Rooney

Wayne Rooney photographed in the aftermath of 'chicken joke' incident

The f***in' chicken better not cross the f***in' road when I'm on the other side the f***in little b*****d f***ing f***er.

Brian Clough

If God had wanted chickens to cross roads he'd have put corn in the tarmac.

Ron Atkinson

Spotter's badge, Clive. For me, Chicko's popped up at the back stick, little eyebrows, and gone bang! And I'll tell you what – I've got a sneaking feeling that this road's there to be crossed.

Ruud Gullit

I am hoping to see some sexy poultry.

Gordon Strachan

I'm really proud of the little fella. Let's face it, if it had been one of the big chickens everyone would be saying how well he'd done, but as it's just one of the wee chickens – it must be luck.

John Gregory

Two months ago that chicken was saying he was happy here. Now he tells me he wants to cross the road. I feel like shooting him.

Kevin Keegan

OK, so the chicken's dead, but I still feel, hey, he can go all the way to the other side of the road.

Bobby Robson

Goose, what? Turkey? Is there a duck here? Where am I?

VALUES AND IDEALS

WINNING ISN'T EVERYTHING

SON MES QUE UN CLUB
(MORE THAN A CLUB)
By **Benedict Paul Gerard Vincent Keane**

10 EX-FOOTBALLERS IN POLITICS
11 POLITICAL GESTURES
7 PETTY REGULATIONS
10 FAILED SAMPLES (THE DRUG TESTS DON'T WORK)
6 SAINTS PLUS 6 SAINTLY SONGS
BIBLICAL XI
10 CHEATS

SON MES QUE UN CLUB (MORE THAN A CLUB)

Benedict Paul Gerard Vincent Keane explains why, no matter where in the world he finds himself, there's always a team to support

I neither support the team from where I was born, nor from where I was brought up or live now. I do not support any one team. A new day, a new team, though always in addition to, rather than at the expense of, any of the other teams that have, over the years, found their way into my affection. The prerequisite for my everlasting support is simple – the club must have a philosophy, a history and a culture that strikes a chord with me. Amidst all the blandness of this superficial age – where strongly held opinions are eyed with suspicion – there is still, it seems to me, the capacity at the very best football matches to be part of a shared creed, to be witness to a visceral, irrational belief amongst the faithful. Football – *pace* Bill Shankly – may or may not be as important as religion but they certainly have a lot in common.

I suppose what I am really saying is that I am on the side of the angels. I support the supporters. Players come, players go, but the supporters are always there with their chants, their colours and most importantly, their ingrained views, prejudices and beliefs. Beliefs which, in many instances, are shaped by where they originate from, and what their club represents; their team becoming the living embodiment of these abstract emotions. When this happens, when the club has become 'more than a club' then, for me, the potential for a certain empathy is irresistible. Elsewhere in this book George Szirtes has described one aspect of this – how Manchester United and the legacy of Munich captured the imagination of a young Hungarian refugee. I feel the same, but in a more specific way. I am a leftward-leaning Roman Catholic (if that is not a contradiction in terms) of Irish extraction. I can be drinking in a certain type of bar in Glasgow, Paris, Barcelona, Dublin or Rome and know that I am with my sort. I have been brought up with the same ideals as them, I carry the same baggage as them, a baggage whose source only those of us who have it know, and the effect, for good or for bad, that it has; a baggage that deep down, I know I do not wish to be rid of.

When Jack Charlton returned to Dublin after Ireland's glorious departure from the 1990 World Cup he said something which moved me greatly. The very essence of the Irish team, he said, was exactly that which people laughed at. These were men from Millwall, Merthyr, Motherwell, anywhere and everywhere, who were only able to play for the Republic because of a grandmother here, a great-grandfather there. But Charlton, newly-anointed as an honorary Irishman himself, reminded them of Ireland's tragedy, that it was a nation of emigrants. His team, as it were, was the diaspora come home; children, grandchildren and great-grandchildren, all, as my father used to say, with the 26 counties on their faces. It is those historical, cultural and political ideals and values that engage me on the terraces. I can watch an Old Firm game and feel at one with any Celtic supporter – this is my tribe where, metaphorically if not literally, I come from. I can watch a Barcelona vs Real Madrid game and know instinctively whose side I am on, that I am at one with the Catalans, that they represent my beliefs and have values and ideals over and above just a sense of place, however important that may be; that in the history and culture of *their* football club, passed from generation to generation, is the universal struggle for identity, to be independent and free. The point is this: to walk into Parkhead into a sea of green, the Camp Nou and a blanket of maroon, to hear the strains of *The Fields of Athenry* is an experience that will find an echo on a dirt pitch in Malta – I know which team I support by the colour of shirt on their backs and the scarves round the necks of their followers. *Athletic Bilbao* vs Espanyol, *Hibs* vs Hearts, *Portugal* vs Germany, the *Republic of Ireland* vs Anyone: all of these sides will have my undying support. They have something of my soul, something that alas my local team, Norwich City, can never have.

10
EX-FOOTBALLERS
IN POLITICS

No weah, ref!

1. GEORGE WEAH

Weah announced his intention to stand
in the 2005 presidential election in his
native Monrovia, having been the subject
of a petition urging him to run. During a
contentious campaign, the Monrovian Inquirer
warned that, 'Mr Weah's soccer colleagues
point to his intolerance for dissent in opinion,

stating that his leadership in Lone Star (nickname of the Monrovian national team) was nothing less than a dictatorship, where disagreement with the captain was intolerable.' When he lost the election to Ellen Johnson-Sirleafin, the Weah camp were quick to make allegations of ballot tampering, intimidation and harassment, though international observers took the view that the election was broadly free and fair. The president of the football federation, however, was desperate to reinstate him, what with Ukraine being on the verge of their first-ever World Cup qualification, and took the matter to court. A judge subsequently ruled that Blokhin could indeed manage the country and be a parliamentarian at the same time, so less than a month later he was restored to the bench. Ukraine became the first European side (after host country, Germany) to qualify for the 2006 World Cup.

2. **Recep Tayyip Erdogan**

A former semi-professional footballer, Erdogan is now the Prime Minister of Turkey.

3. **Ian Gibson**

The Labour MP for Norwich North enjoyed a career that included spells at Airdrie, St Mirren and Queen of the South. Norwich City fan Gibson co-manages and plays for the APPFC – All Party Parliamentary Football Club.

4. **Albert Gudmundsson**

The one-time Arsenal player returned to his native Iceland and ran for president in 1980, but lost.

5. Henry McLeish

The former First Minister of Scotland once turned out for East Fife, for whom he signed after a spell at Leeds United. A talented footballer, McLeish also represented Scotland as a youth international.

6. Pele

Served as Minister of Sport for Brazil between 1995 and 1998. In response to the question 'How do you think futebol should impact in general on society?' the greatest player of all time gave this answer:

'I think futebol is a sport which brings people together as well as instils discipline. Futebol has a big responsibility to society. It can be used to take kids from the streets and away from drugs. You can look to Japan, Africa, China and other parts of the world and see great players, but what is more important is how futebol has developed these men in their personal life. As such it is the type of sport which should be passed down to each generation of children.'

7. Socrates

In the early '80s the Brazilian doctor commanded the midfield for the national side, during the World Cups of '82 and '86. At club level he led a squad while playing at Corinthians that raised eyebrows as it broke with tradition in Brazilian clubs, demanding more open and respectful relations between players and management – the group became known as 'Democracia Corinthiana', at a time when public, democratic initiatives of any kind were of vital importance in Brazil, during the final years of the military regime that ruled the country for 21 years until 1985. The doc was also a member of the Workers' Party.

8. **Oleg Blokhin**

On ending his playing days in 1997, the Dynamo Kiev and Soviet Union legend became a Communist member of the Ukrainian parliament, and in 2003 he was appointed as the country's national coach. The political opposition claimed such a dual mandate was illegal, so in March 2004 Blokhin resigned.

9. **Marc Wilmots**

The Belgian international was another ex-player to mix football and politics simultaneously, but with less success than Blokhin. The Liberal senator was sacked as manager of First Division side St Truiden in February 2005 after barely 10 months in the job.

10. **Zico**

The dead-ball specialist was briefly Minister of Sport for Brazil following his retirement in 1990. He was author of a law, called *Lei Zico*, which regulates the contracts between clubs and players.

11 POLITICAL GESTURES

1. **England's Fascist Salute**

England's friendly international against Germany in 1938 was never designed to be an exercise in sporting endeavour. With the British Prime Minister Neville Chamberlain's appeasement policy in full swing and Hitler's army newly ensconced in Austria, the fixture was designed to demonstrate that Germany was not – yet – an international pariah. Before the game, Foreign

Office officials informed the English players that they would be expected to perform a fascist salute to the crowd, even though Hitler was not at Berlin's Olympic Stadium. The side had made a similar gesture before a game with Italy in Rome five years previously, in recognition of Benito Mussolini's right-wing regime, and had been applauded by the Italian supporters. Team captain Eddie Hapgood is reported to have told the officials to 'stick the Nazi salute where the sun doesn't shine' but the team, which included Stanley Matthews, duly performed their uncomfortable duty before kick-off. The moment provoked outrage in the British press and relegated the match – which finished 6–3 in the visitors' favour – to little more than a footnote.

2. Robbie Fowler and the Liverpool Dockers

The Toxteth Terrier was reported in 2005 as being the wealthiest sportsman in Britain, with a fortune estimated at £28 million through his interests in property and racehorses. 'Red' Robbo had demonstrated his man-of-the-people credentials by illustrating his support for the Liverpool dockers in 1997. The Mersey Docks and Harbour company had locked out their employees after a pay and working practices dispute. When the dockers went on strike Fowler celebrated the scoring of Liverpool's first goal of their UEFA Cup quarter-final against SK Brann by pulling up his shirt to reveal a mock Calvin Klein T-shirt bearing the legend *Support the saCKed Liverpool dockers*. UEFA fined Fowler £900 for his troubles. Ironically, only two days earlier Fowler had received a fax from Sepp Blatter in which the FIFA president praised the way he had tried to encourage the referee to reverse a decision awarding him a penalty in a game against Arsenal at Highbury, when he told the official, in vain, that he had not been fouled by opposing goalkeeper David Seaman.

3. **Internazionale and the Mexican Rebels**

In 2004 Inter donated €5000 (£3500) to Zapatista rebels in Chiapas, southern Mexico. Inter's Argentinian captain Javier Zanetti talked the club into donating money from players' fines after reading of an attack by government forces. 'We believe in a better, unglobalised world enriched by the cultural differences and customs of all the people', Zanetti wrote. Inter have continued to build links with the Zapatistas by funding sports, water and health projects in their area of operation in Chiapas.

The Zapatistas are demanding greater autonomy and indigenous rights. Their campaign has been largely peaceful since January 1994, when at least 150 people died in clashes.

4. **The Basque Derby**

The fixture between Athletic Bilbao and Real Sociedad takes place in a full-blooded but friendly(ish) atmosphere for a local derby. This is because these two hate Spain (Madrid) more than they do each other. Athletic still field only Basques (Sociedad moderated the same policy in 2005, allowing in foreign players, most contentiously, Spaniards). During the Franco dictatorship, Basque team selection was a political act and supporting the clubs was a way of declaring Basqueness in opposition to the loathed centralised Spanish ideology. In 1976, the year after Franco died, José Angel Iribar and Iñaxio

Kortabarria, the respective captains of Athletic and Sociedad, carried the banned Basque flag – the green, red and white Ikurriña – onto the pitch as a symbol of the changing times.

5. Mark Bosnich and the Nazi Salute at White Hart Lane

In the 1996–97 season, then Aston Villa 'keeper Mark Bosnich attracted considerable disapprobation when he gave a Nazi salute in response to abuse from supporters of Tottenham Hotspur, who are well-known for the large Jewish element in their following. It was a joke, of course, and many of Bosnich's best friends are black, and his agent is Jewish etc. But a little further reading casts the Australian's world view in a peculiar light. He suggests that he was kicked out of Manchester United by Labour supporter Sir Alex Ferguson for non-footballing reasons. (Note the unusual role played by Roy Keane in the following account.)

'It was a personality thing – we are very similar characters. I think it was because I was right wing in politics and he was left wing. I think that is why he didn't like me. He wanted all communists in his team. We talked politics a couple of times and we fell out big style. I remember arguing about Maggie Thatcher. I am a big fan and he wasn't. He said she ruined the country. I said she was the best leader since Churchill. We had a massive row after a game at Sunderland and he was late getting on the bus because he had been meeting Tony Blair. I must have said something sarcastic to start it and it got so heated Roy Keane stepped in as peacemaker.'

6. **Sasa Curcic Protests against NATO Bombings**

In March 1999 Crystal Palace played Bradford City in a second tier fixture at Selhurst Park. Only days before, NATO had launched bombing raids on Sarajevo in response to the Serb government's ethnic cleansing campaign and the ousting of Albanians from nearby Kosovo. Sasa Curcic, whose family lived in the city, and his compatriot Gordan Petric, were left out of the Palace side by the manager Steve Coppell on compassionate grounds. Ten minutes before kick-off, the midfielder paraded around the stadium waving a sign which demanded an end to the NATO assaults.

Curcic was (unusually) applauded by the Palace crowd, who remember him more for this incident and a plaited goatee beard rather than for any magic on the pitch. His post-Palace career went into decline, including spells playing Major League Soccer with Metrostars in America, and with Scottish outfit Motherwell. On his eventual retirement, this singular Serb said, 'I would not sign for another club, not even if I was offered $15 million. However, it would be different if they were instead to offer me 15 different women from all around the world.'

7. **Barcelona and Castilian Spain**

In 1925, the Barcelona crowd booed the Spanish national anthem, prompting the country's dictator, General Primo de Rivera, to close the stadium. Eleven years later troops under the control of the fascist leader General Franco shot dead the club's president Josep Sunyol. Things got worse following Franco's victory in the Spanish civil war, with measures against Barcelona taken to new extremes. The Barca squad, fearing for their lives given their iconic status among Catalans, fled to South America, where it subsequently broke up.

In 1943 one of Barca's defining moments saw them win the first leg of a cup semi-final 3–0 against their fierce rivals from the capital. Moments before the start of the second leg, the Barca players were visited in their dressing room by members of Franco's secret police, and told that they could expect severe sanctions, including deportation, if they upset Franco's favourites. Real won the game 11–1.

8. **European Championship Withdrawals**

The idea of a European championship dates back to 1927, when French football chief Henri Delauney presented the proposal to world governing body FIFA. It was not until after the foundation of European governing body UEFA in 1954 that the tournament became a reality. In 1960, the inaugural championships saw Spain drawn to play USSR at the quarter-final stage. The Spanish, still under the control of Franco, withdrew due to conflicting political ideologies and the USSR were awarded a walkover. In 1966 Greece too withdrew, refusing to play neighbouring Albania in the first round: the two nations had been at war for the previous 50 years. In 1992, 10 days before the start of the tournament, the Danish team was asked to participate as a late replacement for Yugoslavia, who had been banned by the United Nations due to the Balkan crisis. Denmark took their bye into the finals and ended up lifting the Henri Delauney trophy after defeating Germany 2–0 in the final in Gothenburg.

9. Wearing the Wrong Shirt Sponsor

In March 2005 Robert Pires had a substantial fine imposed on him by the French FA for making a commercially incorrect gesture by wearing the wrong shirt during an interview while on international duty. The Arsenal midfielder was photographed wearing a Puma shirt when France were sponsored by Adidas. Pires was pretty peeved by the size of the punishment and was entitled to wonder if the world had gone mad in the light of this table of fines:

i) Hurling racist abuse at black footballer: £2000

Spanish manager Luis Aragones' fine for his race attack on Thierry Henry in the same month.

ii) Giving a Nazi salute at a football match: £7000

Former West Ham striker Paolo Di Canio's punishment for a Nazi salute after a Lazio game in January of the same year.

iii) Giving an interview while wearing a Puma shirt when your national team is sponsored by Adidas: £35,000

10. Cristiano Lucarelli's Ringtone

Livorno's captain is a local lad, hailing from a place called Shanghai near the Livorno docks, and he's an avowed Communist. These are good credentials for the leader of the team whose fans don't just take scarves, replica jerseys and loudhailers to matches, but Che Guevara too. His face, emblazoned on banners and T-shirts, is the chosen signature not just of a club but of a city as strongly associated with the left as any in Italy. The Italian Communist party was founded in the port of Livorno in 1921. The football club is a little older and not so successful. When they won promotion to

Serie A in 2004 they broke a 55-year absence from the elite. Lucarelli likes to stir Italian football's appetite for conspiracy. On a dubious refereeing decision given against his team, he declared, 'They want to put us back down in Serie B for political reasons, because our fans are left wing.' When the authorities called him up to order him to recant, his mobile phone could be heard ringing to the tune of *The Red Flag*.

11. Maradona vs George W. Bush

In 2005 Bush went down to Buenos Aires to the Summit of the Americas hoping for some light relief from political pressures at home. It didn't turn out too good for the President as he was greeted by mass anti-American protests led by Diego Armando Maradona – kitted out in a '*Stop Bush*' T-shirt with the 's' of Bush designed as a swastika   vowing to repudiate the forces of imperialism. A month before the visit, Maradona had

With the Hand of God on your side, that should be child's play

interviewed Fidel Castro on his television show *La Noche del Diez (The Night of the Number Ten)* where he made the pledge to lead the protest.

7 PETTY REGULATIONS

When we were kids the bloke stood next to you could piss in your pocket and there was nothing you could do other than grin and bear it because in those days there was no such thing as a fluorescent orange jacket, ergo there was no such thing as a steward. It seems a long way from there to the situation in which we find ourselves today, where there is to be NO:

1. **Falling asleep**

   When police arrested Middlesbrough fan Adrian Carr for falling asleep during a game in 2003 it highlighted the lack of common sense in football today. Is staying awake all that likely a response to many of the games involving the team in question?

2. **Unnecessary noise** – *from radio sets for example – and behaviour likely to cause confusion or annoyance to any person is not allowed in any part of the ground.*

   Remember to leave your tranny at home, and don't ask anyone any baffling questions.

3. **Entering a stadium while drunk**

   To be honest, it's impossible to watch most lower League football in any other condition.

4. **Drinking alcohol within sight of the pitch**

   Ooh, it might give the players ideas about what to do after the game. Or remind them of how they spent the night before, more like.

5. **Smoking**

   Holding on for dear life, 1–0 up, four minutes time-added, about to record a famous victory over the Arsenal in the FA Cup, the last thing you're going to need is a fag, isn't it.

6. Standing up

Words fail us. Apart from the prat behind shouting 'Sit Down!' as you jump for joy to celebrate a goal.

7. Obscene chanting

Listen, part of the reason we go to matches is to advise people that they are wankers. Now fuck off.

10 FAILED SAMPLES (THE DRUG TESTS DON'T WORK)

1. Adrian Mutu

The Romanian striker was banned for seven months and sacked by Chelsea in October after testing positive for cocaine. Prior to the identification of the drug, Mutu suggested it was a substance designed to enhance sexual performance. A likely story, you may think, but on the other hand in 2004 Mutu *was* photographed by paparazzi having sex with a Romanian porn star, and was also involved in a car chase with Romanian police after refusing to stop, which earned him a driving ban. Following this incident, he was advised to seek psychiatric help because of 'extremely serious personality and maturity issues'. Some Chelsea fans would agree – how could a man who lived this lifestyle play football as if on Mogadon?

2. **Mark Bosnich**

Him again. In 2003 the Australian received a nine-month ban after testing positive for cocaine – he was also sacked by Chelsea. He claimed his drink was spiked in a nightclub the night before a game. 'I know people won't believe me but I want to come clean,' he said. 'I wasn't taking any drugs when I was found guilty by the FA. In 15 years of football I never touched them. But everybody believed that I was into drugs, especially because of my relationship with Sophie (Anderton, his model girlfriend). So one day I thought, fuck it, I'm going to do it. I went to a club, bought a £50 wrap of coke, and brought it home to try. Basically, I cracked. I was angry and bitter and I succumbed to being what everyone said I was: a coke fiend. I reached a stage where I was taking six grams of cocaine a day.' Bosnich said he was shocked into detox when – in a reverse Marvin Gaye – he almost shot his father, mistaking him for a burglar.

3. **Lee Bowyer**

During his time at Charlton the famously chilled-out midfielder was disciplined after testing positive for cannabis. At least Bowyer owned up, 'I feel like I've let myself down, there's no need to do stupid things like that if you want to be a footballer,' he said, thus sparing us all the classic defence much favoured by athletes such as Britain's Olympic gold medallist, Mark Lewis-Francis, and Winter Olympics gold-medal winner, Canadian snow boarder Ross Rebagliati: passive smoking. You'd need to passively inhale the smoke from 16 joints in an unventilated room to register the equivalent blood-reading achieved by toking a one-skinner of your own.

4. **Diego Armando Maradona**
Elected the greatest FIFA soccer player of the twentieth century along with Pele, the England fans' favourite Argentinian ended up looking more like Mr Blobby than a World Cup athlete. Maradona was banned from football for 12 months after testing positive for cocaine in 1991. Then he was banned for another 15 months after testing positive for ephedrine (the 'performance enhancer') during the 1994 World Cup. He tested positive yet again in 1997, resulting in another suspension. Eventually obesity forced him to retire altogether. Coke is more commonly an appetite suppressant – did he sprinkle it on his ice cream? In 2000, Maradona suffered a severe heart attack triggered by a cocaine overdose. Fidel Castro, a fan, invited him to undergo detox in Cuba. After that, Maradona told the world he'd kicked his habit. In 2004, he suffered another severe heart attack triggered by yet another cocaine overdose, and woke up in intensive care in a Buenos Aires hospital. His survival was in doubt, and it made headlines worldwide when his respirator was disconnected and he was able to breathe on his own.

5. **Jaap Stam**
Inter Milan midfielder Stam received backing from

Clarence Seedorf in his battle to overturn a drug ban. Seedorf, Dutch teammate of the former Manchester United player, said he was taken aback that Stam tested positive for the steroid nandrolone and, surprise surprise, believed he might have been the victim of someone spiking his food. 'I don't understand how they could find an illegal substance in Stam with that physique he has,' Seedorf told LazioMania.net. True, you could never artificially create that frame, face and scary stare could you? 'We football players should be suspicious even when we drink a glass of milk,' Seedorf went on, 'As we don't know if someone could have put something in it.' Stam eventually received a three month ban in 2001.

6. **Edgar Davids**

The Spurs and Holland international midfielder failed a random drugs test for nandrolone in 2001 while with Juventus. Seven other Italian league players also tested positive for nandrolone during that season. All were most likely victims of the phantom semi-skimmed spiker, of course. Davids received a four-month ban.

7. **Willie Johnston** (*see also:* **5 Pleas for Help ...** p.157)

The Rangers and West Brom winger was sent home in disgrace after Scotland lost 3–1 to Peru in the 1978 World Cup. Pep pills ('for hay fever') were supposed to be to blame (could these be responsible for all the sendings-off too, or was it the other way round?). Scotland teammate Lou Macari, the former Celtic and Manchester United player, and later Stoke City manager said, 'We got the biggest shock of our lives with Willie Johnston. That sort of thing just didn't exist then.'

8. **Tamas Peto**

Dutch side NAC Breda's Hungarian star Tamas Peto tested positive for norandrosterone – a metabolite of three anabolic steroids – after a Dutch Cup match victory against PSV Eindhoven. He denied it of course, but guess what – miraculously his drink hadn't been spiked! No, Peto went down the Willie Johnston 'hay fever' route, citing hormone changes caused by various surgeries as the reason for the test result. He was banned for 20 games, 10 suspended, although it didn't really count, as he was injured anyway at the time.

9. **Al-Saadi Gaddafi**

The blue-blooded Libyan international, former vice-chairman of the Libyan FA and son of Colonel Muammar Gaddafi, was banned for three months by Italian soccer authorities in 2004 after testing positive for nandrolone. In a further leap of inventive excuse-making, Saadi claimed a doctor had given it to him to combat back pain. After serving his ban, he made his Serie A debut for Perugia as a substitute in a game against Juventus. Gaddafi's appearance was a surprise given that Perugia desperately needed to win the game to have any hope of avoiding relegation. Perugia coach Serse Cosmi defended his decision, saying, 'Gaddafi came on because he is a player and not because any one of us wanted to go into history as the one who first played the son of a head of state in the Italian championship.' Gaddafi was previously a member of the board at Juventus and had been open about his support for the Turin club, even arranging for their Italian Super Cup match with Parma to be played in the Libyan capital Tripoli in 2003. 'I spoke with Saadi during the week and he let me know that his dream was to play against Juventus,' Cosmi said. 'I didn't make any promise but having seen how the game was going, I decided to give him an appearance.' Prior to this fixture, Gaddafi had made two appearances on the bench without actually taking part. Perugia won the match 1–0.

10. Frank McAvennie

In the late 1980s Frank was a high-profile tabloid celebrity as well as a footballer who scored regularly for West Ham and later Celtic. Off the pitch the Scot was a regular fixture on the London party circuit, necking champagne and mixing with actors, pop stars and other blonds (his own natural ginger was highlighted) at Stringfellow's. Cocaine was an inevitable part of this yuppie lifestyle. McAvennie said he wished he'd never tried the drug. Understandable: since his admission in 1994 that he had begun snorting cocaine while still playing football he's had two convictions for possession, and had £100,000 seized by Customs, who said it was going to fund a major drugs deal. McAvennie said that his lowest ebb came when he was on trial at Newcastle Crown Court charged with conspiracy to supply £110,000-worth of ecstasy tablets and amphetamines. Looking at a 10-year stretch if convicted, he spent a month on remand in Durham jail, alongside murderers and paedophiles. He broke down in tears after the jury acquitted him.

6 SAINTS PLUS 6 SAINTLY SONGS

1. **Southampton** (nickname: The Saints, home: St Mary's
   Stadium)
   When the Saints Go Marching In (Tune: trad)
   O when the Saints go marchin' in,
   O when the Saints go marchin' in,
   I want to be in that number
   O when the Saints go marchin' in.

2. **St Mirren** (nickname: The Saints)
   If I Had the Wings of a Sparrow (Tune: Bring Back My
   Bonny)
   If I had the wings of a sparrow,
   If I had the a*se of a crow,
   I'd fly over Greenock tomorrow
   And sh*te on the b*st*rds below.
   Sh*te on, Sh*te on
   Sh*te on the b*st*rds below, below,
   Sh*te on, Sh*te on
   Sh*te on the b*st*rds below.

3. **Exeter City** (home: St James Park, co-founded by the
   St Sidwellian Old Boys in 1904)
   West Country Roads (Tune: Country Roads)
   West Country roads, take me home,
   To the place, where I belong,
   St James Park, to see the City,
   West Country roads, take me home.

4. **Birmingham City** (home: St Andrew's)
   Heeeey heeeey Scousers (Tune: Hey Baby)
   Heeeey heeeey Scousers

Ooo ahhhh,
I wanna knoooooow
Where's my stereo, and my video, and my dvd
And my washing machine.

5. **Newcastle United** (home: St James' Park)

   We Hate Middlesbrough etc (Tune: Land of Hope and Glory)

   We hate Middlesbrough FC
   We hate Sunderland too (they're sh*t)
   We hate Man United
   But Newcastle we love you. *(repeat)*

6. **St Johnstone** (nickname: The Saints)

   The Dundee Family (Tune: The Addams Family)

   Your Sister is your Mother,
   Your Father is your Brother,
   Your Granny is your Lover,
   The Dundee family.
   Diddely dee (clap clap), Diddely dee (clap clap),
   Diddely dee, Diddely dee, Diddely dee (clap clap).
   Your diseases are contagious,
   Your smell is quite outrageous,
   You haven't washed for ages,
   The Dundee family.

BIBLICAL XI

Dennis Herod

Ian St. John   Gifton Noël Williams   Ian Bishop   Danny Pugh

Juan Pablo Angel   Remi Moses   Ari Van Lent

Joseph Desire-Job   Christian Ziege   Gabriel Batistuta

Owned by Jesus Gil, coached by Johnny Metgod and using a Mitre ball, the team play at Vicarage Road where matches are officiated by Uriah Rennie. When a porker turns out for the opposition, their fans sing: who ate all the pious?

10 CHEATS

1. ## The Hand of God

2. ## Leeds United

In the late 1960s and early '70s, the team led by Billy Bremner brought new levels of 'gamesmanship' to football. Under manager Don Revie, Leeds would foul individual opponents in rotation, so that no player would draw the referee's attention and receive a booking. Advanced exponents of verbal sarcastic applause, the team would curse the referee's performance at close quarters, but indirectly. 'He's having a nightmare', they'd say, and on being confronted by the official would respond, 'Not *you* ref, the centre-half.'

3. ## Roberto Rojas

As much a pantomime act as a cheat, Chilean 'keeper Roberto 'Condor' Rojas had a brainstorm as Chile found themselves 1–0 down to Brazil in a vital World Cup qualifier at the Maracanã in 1989. Rojas' plan was to force an abandonment, which could lead to a replay in a neutral venue. At around the 67-minute mark he threw himself into the smoke of a firecracker thrown by a Brazilian fan, which had landed nearby, pulled a razor blade from his glove (no premeditation there) and stabbed himself in the head. After carrying Rojas off the pitch, the Chilean players and coaches refused to return claiming conditions were not safe. The plan backfired; after studying video evidence which showed the firecracker had not made any contact with Rojas, Brazil were awarded a 2–0 win and Chile were out of one World Cup and excluded from the next. Rojas was banned for life and the woman who threw the firecracker from the Tribune was signed up by *Playboy* magazine. In May 2001, FIFA lifted the ban. 'At 43, I'm unlikely to play again,' said Rojas, 'But at least this pardon will cleanse my soul.'

4. Panionios and Dinamo Tiblisi

A 2004 UEFA Cup tie between these two sides saw heavy betting on the Greeks to trail the Georgians at half-time and to win at full-time. Unusual patterns caused British bookies to suspend markets on the game, which amazingly turned out to be 0–1 at half-time and 5–2 at 90 minutes (apparently there had been a good amount of betting on those scores too).

5. Esmond Million

With a name you couldn't make up, Million was part of the betting syndicate that shook English football in the early '60s. The Bristol Rovers goalkeeper was due to be paid £300 to throw a match against Bradford Park Avenue in April, 1963. Instead, he threw away his career. Deep in debt following his move from Middlesbrough, Million had failed to find a buyer for his bungalow back in the north-east, and was trying to hold things together when he received a mysterious phone call asking him to throw a game in return for money. Million agreed to the proposal and received £50 in advance. Unfortunately for him, his teammates played a blinder against Bradford and Rovers were 2–0 up before Million had even touched the ball. He managed to concede two lame goals before half-time but in the second period the Bristol defence were solid and the game finished 2–2.

Million posted back his advance and waited for the consequences, which weren't long coming. At training the following week, Rovers manager Bert Tann accused his goalie of attempting to throw the game. He was eventually charged under the Prevention of Corruption Act, found guilty, fined £50, reported to the FA, and banned for life. Ironically, Million found a buyer for the bungalow a week after the Bradford game.

6. **Haka Valkeakoski and Allianssi Vantaa**

Finnish bookmaking firm *Veikkaus* saw the 8787–1 they were offering on 8–0 snapped up by an unusually large number of punters. The bookies were moved to wonder whether all was as it should be when just such a scoreline happened to be the final result in July 2004. After an investigation, the Finnish FA fined Allianssi €10,000 and their coach Thierry Pister €5000 for 'insufficient preparation for a league match'. A disciplinary committee did not back accusations that the match had been fixed, since they could find no proof.

7. **Rivaldo**

Brazil vs Turkey, World Cup 2002. It's the last second of injury time and you have a corner. You're 2–1 up thanks to a penalty that shouldn't have been, and the opposition is down to 10 men. Millions watch as you are struck tamely on the leg by a ball knocked your way by Hakan Unsal – who is only trying to get you to hurry up and take the bloody corner – ergo, he does *not* blast it as that could result in a time-consuming rebound. So what do you do? Go down more spectacularly than the Titanic clutching your face in agony of course. And afterwards, how do you apologise? By admitting the ball never hurt you, that you just wanted to get the player punished. Still, why should you worry, FIFA will only fine you a bit of loose change (€7000) for your pathetic display of theatricals.

8. **Bruce Grobbelaar**

In 1994 the *Sun* newspaper received material alleging

the former Liverpool 'keeper had been involved in taking bribes to fix matchs. In a hotel room rigged with recording equipment, Grobbelaar talked about throwing at least three games and trying to throw others. For a Liverpool match against Newcastle United in 1993 he said he received £40,000 from a betting syndicate. He was also filmed accepting £2000 as part of a payment for throwing games with his new club, Southampton. Charged with conspiracy to corrupt and match-fixing, he was tried in 1997 (alongside the former Wimbledon goalkeeper, Hans Segers, the former Aston Villa striker, John Fashanu, and a Malaysian businessman, Heng Suan Lim). Grobbelaar pleaded innocence, claiming that what he was actually doing was attempting to obtain evidence of wrongdoing from his business partner before going to the police. By all accounts he gave a courtroom performance as audacious as those he produced on the field. The jury failed to reach a verdict and a retrial was ordered, but once more the jury could not decide. All four were acquitted, and in 1999 the Zimbabwean went on to win an £85,000 libel award against the *Sun*.

Two years later the court of appeal ruled that the tabloid had suffered a miscarriage of justice and overturned the award. Grobbelaar went to the House of Lords, which reinstated the jury verdict but slashed his damages to £1 and ordered him to pay the *Sun*'s huge legal costs. The law lords were not convinced he kept his part of the bargain and let in goals, but said he undermined the integrity of the game by acting 'in a way in which no decent or honest footballer would act'.

9. **Robert Hoyzer**

Germany's 2006 World Cup preparations were not helped by the country's biggest match-fixing scandal going to trial in October 2005, only months before the big Kick Off. The trial centred on referee Hoyzer, who admitted to taking bribes to help fix matches. Suspicions were raised when lowly Paderborn came from 2–0 down to beat former European Cup winners SV Hamburg 4–2 in the German Cup in 2004, in a tie in which there were two debatable penalties and an inexplicable sending-off of Hamburg's star striker. It emerged afterwards that Paderborn's fairytale result was aided by Hoyzer who tearfully admitted to taking €70,000 and a flat-screen television in return for influencing the outcome. As a plea bargain on a lenient sentence, Hoyzer said he would tell the authorities everything he knew – including the names of other players and referees who were bent.

Make your own nomination for this enormous category here.

10. **Arsenal, 1919**

After the 1914–18 war, and the resumption of football fixtures, Arsenal were promoted from the Second Division to the First, at the expense of local rivals Hotspur, despite having only finished fifth in the final pre-war league table. It has been alleged that Arsenal's promotion, on historical grounds rather than merit, was thanks to underhand actions by the then Arsenal chairman Sir Henry Norris. Though firm evidence is sketchy, a passage in *Rebels for the Cause* by Jon Spurling (2004) offers supporting evidence for the case, and an investigation by *Four Four Two* magazine reported that financial irregularities had taken place.

THE ARTS
THE BEAUTIFUL GAME

THEY'VE GOT THE WHOLE WORLD AT THEIR FEET
By **Andy Smith**

ANDY SMITH'S FOOTBALLER TOP 10
10 TATTOOS
TOP 10 FANZINES
12 POP GROUPS NAMED AFTER FOOTBALL TEAMS
15 ALBUM TITLES INSPIRED BY FOOTBALL CLUBS
TOP 5 COMPUTER GAMES

THEY'VE GOT THE WHOLE WORLD AT THEIR FEET

Andy Smith gets faintly nostalgic for the footballer 'disc'

They've Got the Whole World at their Feet was the title of the platter that was 'cut' by the England World Cup Squad in 1986, back in the days when a Hatch/Trent composition was acceptable to the public. Accompanying promo work for the players might include lunchtime interviews on 'Wonderful Radio One' and a night-time appearance on *Wogan*, the whole squad decked out in casual wear and kipper ties as if they were just calling in on the way to a stag do, 18 pints of mild, and a chicken in a basket.

It all went the way of the Austin Allegro, of course, for two reasons: New Order and Sky. The former, as Hornby did with earlier football literature, made sub-standard football-related songs untenable, and the latter, well, we all know what Sky did for football: it gave it exposure and cash. Lots and lots of cash. Before Sky, live football was the exception to the rule, tabloids still devoted more time to match reports than rumours, and footballers led reasonably normal lives, earning reasonably normal money. And so they would jump at an opportunity to do something out of the ordinary. This is how you got Kevin Keegan making not one but two Top of the Pops appearances in the late '70s, with *Head over Heels in Love* and *It ain't Easy*; Pan's People and Peter Powell were there for the taking, and any football star who could hold a note, as well as many who couldn't, took a punt on a sideline in a recording career.

It was 1990 that changed it all, when, in a rare display of musical initiative, the FA commissioned New Order to write the song for that year's World Cup anthem. Fans were stunned to hear a proper tune with proper lyrics sung by proper pop stars. Sure, the squad got to sing along to the chorus, and John Barnes was allowed his famous 'Barnes rap', but in the main, the players were restricted to displaying their skills on the video. From *World in Motion* onwards, the footballer as pop star was a species whose days were numbered. The FA learnt its lesson, and turned to pop stars for official tournament songs in future. The best of these, 1996's *Three Lions* proved so popular it became a bona fide terrace chant in its own right, which is some achievement considering that Baddiel & Skinner were involved (as well as the Lightening Seeds' Ian Broudie). Not all efforts were as successful; anyone remember Echo and the Bunnymen's collaboration with the Spice Girls for France 1998?

Now that Sky has made millionaires of even the most average top-flight player and given him access to everything he could ever want – a huge packet for modelling Y-fronts, girls going weak at the knees just for his *celebrity* – he has no need to embarrass himself with an appearance on CD: UK. Twenty years ago, footballers could only sing about having the world at their feet; now, with the money already in the bank, the garage full of Ferraris, the *Hello* centre spreads, they don't need to sing about it because it's already their reality. If they feel a need to be close to the musical heartbeat, the safer route is the one established by David

Beckham, Jamie Redknapp and Ashley Cole, to name but three – marry a popstar, let the missus' vocal chords take the strain.

ANDY SMITH'S
FOOTBALLER
TOP 10

Even worse than Robson and Jerome

1. GLENN & CHRIS
Diamond Lights

The greatest. Mullets, flecked jackets with
rolled-up sleeves, a dancy 'thing' and a terrible
song. The follow-up single was called 'It's
Goodbye'. 'Nuff said. But they were both
geniuses on the pitch, so we can forgive.

2. **Owen Paul** – *You're My Favourite Waste of Time*
Gave up promising football career (the young Scotsman was apprenticed to Celtic, when he caught a whiff of Sid Vicious and thought 'I want some of that!'), got this song to number 3, gave up promising music career. Genius.

3. **Kevin Keegan** – *It Ain't Easy*
Neither is listening to it, Kevin. Nice shirts though.

4. **Andy Cole** – *Outstanding*
The only thing outstanding about this is surely the debt he owes to society for it.

5. **Paul Gascoigne** – *Fog on the Tyne*
Football genius goes to World Cup, cries, and comes back a hero. A nation feels its sympathy start to wane on hearing this version of the Geordie classic.

6. **Terry Venables** – *Bye Bye Blackbird*
One day, thought Terry, I'll own a nightclub, not sing in one. Thank the lord he was right.

7. **Ian Wright** – *Do the Right Thing*
Amazingly this was produced by the Pet Shop Boys' Chris Lowe. Nice try, but not enough to stop it being rubbish.

8. **Jeff Astle** – *Sweet Water*
Creditable cover of Richard Clayderman hit that doesn't quite exonerate him for his miss in Mexico in 1970.

9. **Ron Atkinson** – *Let's Give Love a Try*
Even as a Christmas novelty record this is only scraping the Top 10.

10. **Vinnie Jones** – *Woolly Bully*

Footballer, actor, musician and hardman. It's great.

10 TATTOOS

With far fewer sailors about than there used to be when the Navy ruled the waves, professional footballers have joined forces with rappers to save tattoo parlours from liquidation.

1. David Beckham

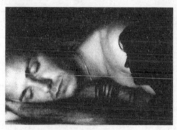

A super slo-mo action replay of all the needlework: *David*, a video portrait of the sleeping footballer, by Sam Taylor-Wood, shown in the National Portrait Gallery in 2004.

His frame hosts a mass of images and messages – a crucifix on his back to look over the names of his children, an angel to watch over the crucifix, a cherub and an angel on his right arm and shoulder, a Hindi tattoo down his left forearm that misspells the name of his wife, Victoria (with an 'h' as in Vihctoria), and the Roman numeral VII in which he does a little better by correctly identifying his Manchester United squad number.

2. Freddie Ljungberg

The Swedish and Arsenal forward and part-time model provoked a debate about the safety of tattoos when news emerged that one on his back nearly wrecked his career after becoming infected. Freddie (a former leading exponent of the *red* quiff, incidentally) underwent tests for AIDS and cancer as doctors tried to establish the reason for his persistently inflamed hip. After two weeks of examinations they realised that the player was experiencing a rare allergic reaction to the ink used in the two tattoos of panthers on his back.

3. **Robbie Savage**

As we already know, Alan Birchenall sums Savage up as follows, 'If brains were chocolate he wouldn't have enough to fill a Smartie.' Savage helps confirm this assessment by buying a banana-coloured Ferrari, and sporting a tattoo of the Armani logo.

4. **Baichung Bhutia**

The tattoo on his right arm – a meticulously imprinted picture of footballer in action – speaks of Baichung's intense love of football. The Sikkimese became the first Indian footballer to sign a professional contract with a club in Europe, when he was transferred from East Bengal Club, Kolkatta to Second Division-club Bury FC (in the Greater Manchester area) in 1999. After the 2001/02 season Bhutia decided to return to India to play for Mohun Bagan AC – the Indian National Football League (NFL) champions 2001/02. A year later he was back with East Bengal. When Baichung was a kid he would scan newspapers to see if there was any football match being aired on TV, and if so he would take a three-hour bus ride from his native Tinkitam to Gangtok to watch the matches, as his own village had no television sets.

5. **Vinnie Jones**

The Welsh international hardnut, recording artist and specialist gangster-movie actor, describes his body gallery in his own words:

i) Firstly I have a simple rose on my left forcarm. Classic.

ii) I then marked my achievement of winning the FA Cup, with Wimbledon in 1988, with this FA Cup tattoo on the outside of my right leg.

iii) Having helped Leeds to the Second Division Championship in 1989/90, I got their rose on the outside of my left leg, to neatly balance the FA Cup on the other leg. Sixty pounds well spent.

iv) Getting the captaincy for Wales was such a proud moment for me, I really felt like the governor. This warranted another tattoo, a beauty put on my chest – the dragon and the feathers. It took three hours and cost £150. This tattoo will definitely last as long as my pride at becoming captain.

v) And last but by no means least, with the greatest thanks to my immediate family, for all they have done for me, supporting me through thick and thin, Tanya, Aaron & Kaley, in the middle of my shoulders.

6. **Christian Vieri**

The striker falls into the category of those many, possibly apocryphal, tales of people who wander into tattoo parlours, choose a few Chinese symbols that take their fancy, and some time later finding that they are sporting the legend *'I is really a very dim boy'* down their forearm. Vieri, who held the mantle of most expensive player in the world when he left Lazio for Inter for £32m in 1999 (a fee branded 'disgusting' by the Vatican), admitted to this approach, picking his Chinese tattoos based on their appearance. It seems he is as fortunate in random tattoo selection as he is in picking up signing-on fees. The meaning of his marks are: constant, regular, persistent, thunder; clan, family, mister, heart, mind, intelligence, soul; harmony, peace, peaceful, calm.

7. **Marc Bircham**

In a classic case-history of bad timing, the then Millwall (nickname, The Lions) player got a big lion tattoo on his arm. Just six months later he was released by the club. Bircham, who claims to be a lifelong QPR fan, and who also favours ludicrous blue guano-like hairstyles, went on to become the subject of the song, *He's got a Lion on his arm, he's got birdshit on his head,* in future fixtures between the clubs.

In a similar vein, there is the story about a Newcastle fan who got a caricature tattoo of Andy Cole embroidered on his leg *one* week before Cole transferred to Manchester United. Let this be a lesson to us all; just stick to the club crest, okay, it's the *only* safe lifelong-affiliation tattoo: when Julie has long since gone, Hamilton Academicals will always be there.

8. **Djibril Cissé**

Another player with many markings. The French striker says that his tattoos speak of his gentleness, they include the names of everyone he has ever loved. On his neck is Ilona, his daughter's name, and spread across his back are huge wings: in Islam Djibril was an angel who dictated the Koran to Muhammad, 'Djibril means Gabriel', Cissé explains.

9. **Maradona**

Has a tattoo of Che Guevara on his shoulder and of Fidel Castro on his leg.

10. 'No dissertations from you about tattoos or whatever tonight, eh Eamon?'

'No, Bill, but I know where Beckham's tattoo came from.'

'No libel on air, Eamon, please.'

'I'll tell you later then.'

Bill O'Herlihy and Eamon Dunphy nearly talking tatts for Irish broadcaster RTE during Euro 2004.

TOP 10 FANZINES

Martin Smith is editor of *The Oatcake*, the Stoke City fanzine which started in 1988 during the fanzine explosion of that era. *The Oatcake* is probably on the highest issue-number of any fanzine, having passed 400 and has won several awards from football magazines. Martin, who is one of the more handsome and worldly-wise of all fanzine editors, selects ten of the best.

1. **When Saturday Comes**

It seems a long, long time ago since I first picked up a copy of *WSC* and as far as longevity goes there's nothing to compare with this national football fanzine. It may have sold its soul to the advertisers a long time ago, but it's an acceptable trade-off if you want something decent to read about football in general. Although *WSC* does devote many pages to the stuff you read about in the tabloids it's still the only publication to truly cover football on every level, and I've learned more about non-league and overseas football from *WSC* than from any other source down the years. Long may it continue to survive.

2. **Red Issue** (Manchester United)

Despite the natural instincts of many football supporters to dislike/despise Manchester United you still have to tip your hat to a fanzine that has had more original ideas in the pages of one issue than some other publications manage in several years. A hugely entertaining read, provided you're not of the 'Scouse' persuasion!

3. **Brian Moore's Head Looks Uncannily Like London Planetarium** (Gillingham)

As well as having the best-ever title of a football fanzine *BMHLULLP* also provided me with the best laugh I've ever enjoyed from a fanzine – the story being the one of the Gills supporter who travelled to a pointless away-game wearing his Gillingham shirt and denim jacket and realised with some despair, after seeing his reflection in a shop window, that the only part of the Zanussi sponsor's panel you could see on his shirt, between the opening of his jacket, was 'anus'. You couldn't make it up.

4. **The Northern Light** (Aberdeen)

Probably the funniest and most vitriolic of all fanzines ever. The target of their humour and hate were Graeme Souness' Glasgow Rangers and the cartoons and original jokes were of the highest order. The early issues should be an essential part of any fanzine fancier's collection.

5. **The Leyton Orientear** (Leyton Orient)

One of the great joys of the early days of fanzines was meeting up with the guys from other publications and none were better company than those responsible for the excellent 'Orientear'. In person and in print they typified the genuine and unconditional love of supporters for a lower league club.

6. **King of the Kippax** (Manchester City)

With a style, look and A4 presentation all of its own *KOTK* was one of the most popular of all of the early fanzines and brought its editor, Dave Wallace, to the fore in many of the major issues which surrounded the crisis-torn Maine Road club for so many years. Not all of it cast him in the best light, or won him friends in the stands and terraces, but *King of the Kippax* made its mark.

7. **The Gooner** (Arsenal)

The first fanzine I ever saw, apart from our own, and one whose 40-plus pages made me realise how poorly produced my own early 12-page efforts really were. With an excellent mix of humour, serious comment and historical offering *The Gooner* was always one of the fanzines I would actively seek out on my visits to the fanzine shelves at Select-a-Disc in Nottingham.

8. **The Voice of the Valley** (Charlton Athletic)

In these days of widespread Football Trust participation in our game it's worth remembering the pioneering and groundbreaking efforts of *VOTV*. They never accepted Charlton's exile from their spiritual home and fought tirelessly to get their club back to where it belonged, even to the point of standing in local elections on just such a platform. Hardly a laugh a minute as fanzines go but probably the worthiest one I've ever read.

9. **Wise Men Say** (Sunderland)

WMS was easily one of the better efforts to emerge from the pack during the fantastic fanzine explosion of the mid- to late-'80s and seemed set to go on to greater and greater things. However, at the very height of their success they pulled the plug and got out, claiming that fanzines were becoming too commercial and losing sight of what they were really supposed to be about. How ironic then that the most popular Sunderland fanzine today, the widely admired *A Love Supreme* is also the most commercial of them all!

10. **The City Gent** (Bradford City)

If you're into girth then City Gent is the fanzine for you as its issues would often weigh in at an unbendable 100 A5 pages of eclectic material, ranging from all things Bantam through to essential reviews of Bradford's finest curry houses. To be honest, I used to lose the will to live through some of the more drawn-out, page-filling articles in such a massive issue, but there's no denying City Gent's well-deserved credibility among the higher echelons of the fanzine elite.

12 POP GROUPS NAMED AFTER FOOTBALL TEAMS

1. **Red Star Belgrade**

Hailing from Chapel Hill, North Carolina, this husband-and-wife duo took their name from the once mighty Yugoslav Red Army team. Their debut EP was called,

'Lose Your Temper, Gain An Injury', a record that could be dedicated to many hundreds of players. Make your own selection here.

2. St Germain

Ludovic Navarre, alias Saint Germain, is credited as being the pioneer of the French Touch, the new electronic music of France. Some claim Navarre named his outfit after a well-known pretender in the court of Louis XV in eighteenth-century France, but it seems quite clear that it is in homage to 1996 European Cup Winners, Paris Saint Germain. Online reviewer, **hamid**, from Tehran, says: 'St Germain are a mini funkyard, easy to listen to, I didn't know that French can make such music. Excellent for the whole community of Europa that do not give a damn about the rest of the world. They just want to shake their ass & smoke their joint.'

3. Saint Etienne

Indie survivors and purveyors of sparkling dance pop, the British band named themselves after the French European Cup Runners Up, 1976, because they liked their shirts.

4. Boca Juniors

Sweet Indie popsters from Northwich, Cheshire, in the middle of Olde England. It's an unwritten law of this genre that if you name yourself after a team then you must not live in the country where the team play, or generally have anything to do with them. See also:

5. Dynamo Dresden

Apparently, the band leader of the Welsh 'lounge-core' collective saw Dynamo playing in the UEFA Cup during the '80s and became a fan. Or he remembered their name, at least. And see also:

6. Aston Villa

Hailing from the Paris suburbs, the rock group, who have been a fixture on the French music scene since 1994, remain true to the trope by naming themselves after an overseas team. Formed by Frédéric Franchitti and Hocine Hallef in the early '80s, the five-piece are big football fans who display wacky Gallic GSOH by claiming that their name is also an amalgamation of two icons: the James Bond Aston Martin sports car, and the rebel general of the Mexican Revolution, Pancho Villa.

7. Kaiser Chiefs

The Kaiser Chiefs are without a doubt the most famous South African football team, having picked up more than 63 trophies since 1970 (though they have not won a league title since 1992). Lucas Radebe used to play for them before joining Leeds United. The band are Leeds fans, unfortunately for them, or fortunately, if you've heard them.

8. Wigan's Ovation

Made it to #12 in the hit parade in March 1975 with Northern Soul novelty record 'Skiing in the Snow'. Unpopular with Northern Soul purists who thought that their all-night scene was being badly misrepresented: from the Ovation's appearances on Top of the Pops the general public were left with the impression that Northern Soulsters were a bunch of white guys wearing tight jumpers and ridiculous strides.

9. **Tangerine Dream**

Nicknamed after lower-league English team Blackpool FC, also known as the Seasiders. Tangerine Dream might alternatively have been called *Seaside Dream* and the history of progressive music could be so different. Blackpool's most famous achievement was winning the FA Cup in 1953 in the so-called Matthews Final. Blackpool were 3–1 down to Bolton Wanderers as Stanley Matthews, striving to gain a Cup winners' medal for the first time, at the age of 38, stepped forward to dominate the last quarter of the match. Many people think he scored a hat trick, but it was his mate Stan Mortensen who did that. With three minutes to go Matthews put in a trademark dribble to the byline and cut the ball back for Bill Perry to score the dramatic winner to make it 4–3 at the final whistle.

10. **Liverpool Express**

Ex-Merseybeat Billy Kinsley and three friends he had been playing football with over the years – Roger Scott Craig, Tony Coates and Derek Cashin – joined together to create Liverpool Express in 1975. They had several hit records across Europe but their greatest success came in South America where they scored three consecutive Top Ten hits and toured in 1977, one of the first bands to play in the huge sport stadiums in Brazil. Arriving at Rio de Janeiro's Airport, the band was greeted by thousands of hysterical fans. *It was quite a shock for us to be welcomed to Brazil by so many screaming fans. In fact, we thought someone famous was on our flight and we had no clue what was going on,* said Billy about the experience.

11. **Grasshopper and the Crickets**

Named after the Zurich Grasshoppers, or possibly not, Grasshopper and flautist Suzanne Thorpe goof off, get experimental, and deliver some tingly pop music on World Cup concept album, 'Orbit of Eternal Grace.'

12. **The Eagles**

Obscure American Crystal Palace tribute band.

15 ALBUM TITLES INSPIRED BY FOOTBALL CLUBS

1. **Aston Villa**   Aston Villa
2. **London 0 Hull 4**   The Housemartins

A rare away win for the Tigers

3. **Your Arsenal**   Morrissey
4. **Boca Juniors**   Mufflon 5

5.	**Barcelona**	Freddie Mercury with Montserrat Caballé
6.	**Hearts of Stone**	Southside Johnny & the Asbury Jukes
7.	**Boston**	Boston
8.	**Chelsea Girl**	Nico
9.	**Stoke**	Philip Jeck
10.	**Sheep Farming in Barnet**	Toyah Wilcox
11.	**Lincoln**	They Might Be Giants
12.	**Bury The Hatchet**	The Cranberries
13.	**Juve the Great**	Juvenille
14.	**All I want for Christmas is a Dukla Prague Away Kit**	Half Man Half Biscuit
15.	**Life thru a Lens**	Robbie Williams

TOP 5 COMPUTER GAMES

1. **Pro Evo**

Amazing graphics and playability, the true football sim, player likeness is fantastic and the gameplay has improved throughout the series.

Amazing graphics and playability

263

2. **Championship Manager/Football Manager**

   Huge database of players and staff, has gone from
   basic to more advanced artificial intelligence (AI) in
   terms of interaction with the players and media. Purely
   management though. *Football Manager* (SI Games)
   kept the database and *Championship Manager* is a
   poor man's second – the database made the game and
   it lives on with *FM2006* with teamtalks, individual
   training regimes etc.

3. **Kick Off**

   On the Amiga, huge in its day, overhead view, basic
   management based on a small number of attributes,
   minimal transfer scope and imaginary database of
   players. Awful ball control until you got used to it – then
   it was still awful, but you were used to it.

4. **Sensible Soccer**

   A bit better to play and you could transfer real names;
   we always remember Letchkov being cheap but very
   quick with a right curler on him!

5. **FIFA**

   Always good for a laugh but it was more for show, you
   could run up the field with any player and score, shoot
   from 50 yards on target, always pick out a man no
   matter where you passed, etc.

THE MIND AND IDEAS

'HE PLAYS THE FIRST YARD IN HIS HEAD'

WE'RE FOOTBALL PEOPLE, BUT WE'RE ALSO STUDENTS OF LIFE

By **Mark Eltringham**

10 BRAINIACS

10 PHILOSOPHY FOOTBALL T-SHIRT SLOGANS

10 SMOKERS

10 LESSONS AKI RIIHILAHTI LEARNED
IN THE PREMIERSHIP

THE LAND WHERE THE JUMBLIES LIVE – 10
NONSENSICAL THOUGHTS FROM THE MADNESS OF
SELHURST PARK

11 WORDS OF WISDOM

APOLLO XI

WE'RE FOOTBALL PEOPLE, BUT WE'RE ALSO STUDENTS OF LIFE
Mark Eltringham thinks his way through ninety minutes

Given the title, you might think that this is going to be one of those smart-arse pieces which sets out to prove that football offers us some sort of insight into the human condition, illuminated by lots of quotations from famous intellectuals such as (former goalkeeper) Albert Camus[1] and (Bradford City fan) JB Priestly[2] to lend the author a vicarious cerebral credibility. You'd be dead right.

The fact is that there is undoubtedly something about football that speaks to people in a universal language. No other sport, with the possible exception of boxing, has more to say about what makes us human. I know that followers of rugby and cricket like to think they occupy the intellectual high ground, but that is mainly a class thing. The fact is that the only decent quotation about rugby is a comparison with football,[3] as you'd expect from a sport burdened with the inferiority complex of an overshadowed little brother. And cricket appears to have inspired very little in the way of original thought, a state of affairs typified by John Major's trite appeal to an England that bears absolutely no relation to the England I know nor the one I grew up with. [4]

The working man's ballet can even claim the moral high ground, because it is (or was) the sport and cultural focus of the working class. And, as John Rose demonstrates in his book *The Intellectual Life of the British Working Classes*, the working autodidact is a much more attractive figure than his or her advantaged and educated middle-class contemporary. Self-taught or otherwise, rough, straight-talking and passionate about their football, this was the crowd depicted by LS Lowry in *Going to the Match*, his famous painting that fetched £2 million at auction in 2000. These people formed the bulk of the crowd when I first started going to games, in what we now think of as a Golden Age, in the mid-'70s. This was the England and the game I knew, a million miles away from the cosy, mythical Darling Buds England of John Major, yet no less poetic for all that. Sure, it was a dark poetry most of the time and you had to tolerate unromantic things like toilets that swam with piss, but it was magical nonetheless. Something was lost to the game at the same time they sorted out the toilets and Man United started winning things again.

So profound is football's fascination for intellectuals, that individual positions have their own canon. Inevitably the goalkeeper has attracted most interest. Albert Camus himself was a goalkeeper before taking the tiny step to become an existentialist. Nabokov spoke poetically about the goalie's unique role in the game.[5] Wim Wenders went one step further by making a whole film about the existential angst that grips the custodian, *The Goalkeeper's Fear of the Penalty Kick*.

And yet in spite of the weight of thought bearing down on it from the world's foremost intellectuals, artists and philosophers, football remains in many ways an anti-intellectual game for those employed by it. True, the greatest footballers are able to run the first yard in their heads and carry around with them – by all accounts – a detailed mental picture of what is going on all over the pitch, but you have to worry about a sport in which it is possible to be seen as an effete, probably homosexual brainiac by mere dint of reading the *Guardian*, as happened to Graeme Le Saux. I also recall the way in which commentators would explain in awed tones how Brian McClair had 'a degree'. We shouldn't be too surprised at this. When we ask ourselves – as we often do – 'why the hell do I do this?' the player can answer 'because it's my job', whereas the fan's most feasible answer is 'because it's who I am'. That's bound to create an existential crisis from time to time.

As far as the English are concerned, the only exceptions to this distrust of intellectualism among players and managers appear to be when they are French. The French don't have to be Jean Paul Sartre[6] to earn instant intellectual status. This can amuse them when they see Arsène Wengar set on a plinth of erudition simply based on the fact that he looks like a geography teacher. Even more baffling to them is our assumption that Eric Cantona is some sort of free-thinking radical, when to French ears his coarse Marseilles accent and opaque, received musings make him sound like Benny from *Crossroads* reading aloud from Aldous Huxley's *Collected Essays*.

In spite of this, football's place as a source of inspiration for observers of the human condition is assured. Now that the working man is an endangered species, its role as the working man's ballet may be past, but it will continue to be the thinking man's ballet.

Notes

1. 'All that I know most surely about morals and obligations I owe to football.' Albert Camus, quoted in Herbert R Lottman, *Albert Camus*, 1979.

2. 'Through a turnstile into another and altogether more splendid kind of life, hurtling with conflict and yet passionate and beautiful in its art.' JB Priestley, *Good Companions*, 1929.

3. 'Rugby is a beastly game played by gentlemen; soccer is a gentleman's game played by beasts.' Henry Blaha, rugby player, 1972.

4. 'Fifty years on from now, Britain will still be the country of long shadows on cricket grounds, warm beer, invincible green suburbs and dog lovers.' John Major, *Speech to the Conservative Group for Europe*, 22 April 1993.

5. 'The goalkeeper is the lone eagle, the man of mystery, the last defender. Less the keeper of a goal than the keeper of a dream.' Vladimir Nabokov, autobiography, *Speak, Memory*, 1951.

6. 'In football, everything is complicated by the presence of the opposite team.' Jean Paul Sartre, autobiography, *Mots*, 1963.

10
BRAINIACS

Dr Socrates

1. SOCRATES

The Brazilian skipper, midfielder and captain
of the national side at the 1982 and 1986 World
Cups is a qualified doctor, who, in common
with many members of his profession, sees
nothing wrong with the odd fag – he was
reported to smoke at least a pack a day.

2. **Brian McClair**

   The player nicknamed 'Choccy', (because his surname rhymes with chocolate éclair) has a degree in Mathematics. Regarded as one of the greats at Manchester United, he is now their Academy Director.

3. **Tony Galvin**

   Shirt flapping, socks rolled down, the unkempt Spurs midfielder had a tidy enough mind: his degree in Russian came in handy for putting in those telling crosses from the left wing.

4. **Barry Horne**

   The former Welsh international has a degree in Chemistry from Liverpool University.

5. **Steve Coppell**

   Retired from playing with a dodgy knee at the age of 28, Coppell still holds the record for making the most consecutive appearances for an outfield player for Manchester United (206). He has a degree in History, also from Liverpool University.

6. **David Wetherall**

   Not content with scoring the goal that kept Bradford City in the Premiership in the '99/00 season, Wetherall is another with a degree in Chemistry. It's a First too.

7. **Steve Heighway**

   '70s legend at Liverpool – later to join the coaching staff – Heighway's early promise as a winger was not spotted by professional clubs and therefore, being a smart lad, he concentrated on his studies and played in the non-league while completing a degree in Economics.

8. **Iain Dowie**

Another whose early promise went unappreciated (he was told by Southampton to forget about turning professional), Dowie went on to captain Northern Ireland – gaining 56 caps – and has turned out to be an inspirational manager. He applies his qualification in Aeronautical Engineering to his work: 'My degree allows me to be logical, maybe the algebraic approach makes me analytical', he says.

9. **Fabio Pecchia**

Bologna's midfield maestro is a registered accountant who takes off the first Wednesday of every month to file his teammates' tax returns.

10. **Slaven Bilic**

As well as being infamous worldwide for the dive in the 1998 World Cup semi-final which saw French defender Laurent Blanc cautioned and ruled out of the final, the Croatian defender is remembered none too fondly by Evertonians either, many of whom put him in their All-Time Worst XI. So it's just as well he has something to fall back on: a qualification in Law.

10 PHILOSOPHY FOOTBALL T-SHIRT SLOGANS

Philosophyfootball.com advertise themselves as 'sporting outfitters of intellectual distinction'.

1. Imagine people playing football, kicking the ball in the air, chasing, fouling each other. Is there not the case to make up the rules as we go along?
    Ludwig Wittgenstein

2. If there is a goal there must be a system.
    Hegel

3. After literature and sex, football is one of the great pleasures.
    Pier Paolo Pasolini

4. The goal passes through a series of phases independent of the will of man.
    Karl Marx

5. All that I know most surely about morality and obligations, I owe to football.
    Albert Camus

Albert Camus, writer, thinker, smoker and goalkeeper (for the University of Algiers)

6. And so Schwejk opened the door, placed the stern gentleman at it, and gave him a kick worthy of the

shot of the best player in an international football championship.
Jaroslav Hasek

7. It is not just a simple game. It is a weapon of the revolution.
   Che Guevara

8. Each succeeds in reaching the goal by a different method.
   Niccolò Machiavelli

9. Nothing is simultaneously freer and more constrained than the action of the good player. He quite naturally materialises at just the place the ball is about to fall, as if the ball were in command of him – but by that very fact, he is in command of the ball.
   Pierre Bourdieu

10. Power is only too happy to make football bear a diabolical responsibility for stupefying the masses.
    Jean Baudrillard

10 SMOKERS

If you are a smoker and smoking is still allowed in your stadium, you'll know that nothing soothes and focuses the mind during the 90 minutes like 20 B&H. For a manager, cigarettes can bring trophies too:

1. **Cesar Luis Menotti** (Argentina coach)
   The undisputed archetype of the tortured gaffer who lives purely on nerves, caffeine and soft packs of

Camel. With the aspect of a less healthy Nick Cave, the Argentinian coach burned his way through carton after carton as he haunted the touchline chain-smoking while guiding his country to victory in the 1978 World Cup on home soil.

2. **Klaus Toppmöller** (Bayer Leverkusen coach)

Came to prominence during Leverkusen's extraordinary run to the 2002 Champions League final. Memorably described by BBC commentator Jon Champion as having 'hair like David Gower and dress-sense like Austin Powers', Klaus was an old-school smoker for whom every match was a game of two packs. After holding Manchester United 1–1 in the semi-final second leg at the Bay Arena, and consequently going through on away goals (it had been 2–2 in the first leg at Old Trafford), Herr Toppmöller advised the fans that, 'Now is the time to drink, smoke and find women.' Somehow, you can't quite hear Sir Alex Ferguson saying that.

3. **Johan Cruyff** (ex-Barcelona manager)

A triple bypass was the ultimate consequence for the great Dutchman who routinely went through 40 a match in his time in charge at the Nou Camp, where he could be observed pacing the line like an overactive *flic* in a French movie.

4. **Stan Ternent** (ex-Burnley, ex-Gillingham manager)

Face like a bag of spanners, Embassy Regal cuffed in palm of hand, nails like talons. Old-school, rude boy: they don't make 'em like this anymore. Stan's idea of a training regime consists of ten pints, a fight and a leg-over, none of this new-fangled namby-pamby running around little cones on the ground, drinking milk and eating pasta nonsense.

5. **Malcolm Allison** ('70s Manchester City manager)
   If you're going to knock about wearing a fedora, it'd look silly without an 18-inch Havana to go with it.

6. **Gianluca Vialli** (Chelsea and Watford coach)
   To enhance his sulking technique, Luca was seen pulling on a Marlboro Light as he was left on the bench during his later playing days at Chelsea. On a further drug-related note, Vialli became Cockney rhyming slang for Columbia's principal export: Gianluca Vialli = Charlie = cocaine.

7. **Daniel Passarella** (Argentina manager)
   As captain of the World Cup-winning side in 1978 and beyond, Passarella won many honours in the game, including several league championships with River Plate, the club he served for most of his career. But the highlight was, of course, to lift the Jules Rimet trophy on home turf (the final itself was played on Passarella's home ground, Estadio Monumental), under Menotti's guidance, and to enjoy many a World Cup winner's post-match fag with him afterwards. If you study Passarella's touchline chain-smoking technique you can see the influence – the choreography is matched drag for drag.

8. **Derek Dougan** (Wolverhampton Wanderers legend)
   'The Doog' took a lateral approach to weaning his fellow pros off the fags in the '70s, as Stoke skipper *Peter Dobing* explains. 'Derek Dougan put me onto a pipe when we both played for Blackburn Rovers. Derek was very much a trend-setter in those days. Until then I

had only smoked cigarettes ... but I've not touched one since. You get far more satisfaction out of a pipe, as any pipe man will tell you. It certainly helps me relax after matches.'

9. **Paul Gascoigne** (Maestro and manager manqué)

Gazza was unmasked as a serial puffer during his fat period before World Cup 1998. However Glenn Hoddle, the England manager at the time, decided to take a softly, softly approach. 'Paul's been smoking since he was in Rome with Lazio, six or seven years,' he said. 'If I tried to stop him for three weeks now, it might have an adverse effect. Ossie Ardiles was on 40-a-day when he won the World Cup with Argentina, and there's a fellow called Gianluca Vialli at Chelsea too,' Hoddle added, warming to his theme. 'It didn't bother Ossie and it doesn't bother me.'

10. **Lee Bowyer** (Professional Bad Lad)

One of a left-field group of players to have tested positive for cannabis, in Bowyer's case the chillin' effect is very hard to locate. Once the most expensive teenager in English football with his £2.8m move from Charlton to Leeds United, Bowyer's latter-day record includes court appearances for violence and a month-long club ban by Newcastle United following an on-pitch scrap with fellow Newcastle player Kieron Dyer. The midfielder tends to comes on more Smokin' Joe Frazier, than Lee Scratch Perry.

10 LESSONS AKI RIIHILAHTI LEARNED IN THE PREMIERSHIP

The Finnish International, who gives his occupation as 'Motor of Midfield', on his idiosyncratic website (www. akirihilahti.com), played in the English top-flight with Crystal Palace in the 04/05 season. The following was a May, 2005 entry to the site:

It's a different world, you can do whatever you like now, your life will never be the same again.' This is what everyone said when we got promoted to the Premiership. I feel a bit cheated because it's been nine months, yet the story is still the same: I can see from the mirror the same old ugly duckling. The Premiership doesn't make you a beautiful swan. Fairytale or not, it teaches you many things. What are the differences? I've often been asked. Probably many. But here are at least 10 things I have learned in the Premiership.

1. **You get punished harshly.**

    Don't miss-kick it or give away a half chance, don't be out of shape even for a second, never lose your concentration. Mistakes are not human in the Premiership, they are crucial. You just can't get away with anything, there are no second chances. So many times we have felt we've played well and been as good as the opponent but have still left with nothing. Unlucky is not a word you like or believe anymore when you hear it too often. Eighty-nine minutes of good play counts for nothing, any one situation can crucify you. That is why a Premiership striker costs so much more than Sunday-league wannabes, because he delivers every day of the week.

2. **'Don't you know who I am?' won't get you into nightclubs.**

   I was told that the Premiership status would open every door. Maybe my name or face are too difficult, but people are not even giving me a second look. Me neither. I don't think and don't even want to know if the 'I'm a Premiership player' card works. There are no other privileges either: parking attendants don't respect your higher-division status and mercilessly clamp your car and you have to queue in the supermarkets as normal. So don't believe anything about the *Footballers' Wives* programme.

3. **Team shape and defending are crucial.**

   Even the champions, Chelsea, base their game on this, actually are best at it. You need to be a compact unit, you need to have a good team shape and game plan in the most competitive modern football, and it all has to start from defending if you want to succeed. Not conceding goals makes your season. The inventive, lovely and attacking pure football is not likely to win anymore, it remains an admirable Utopia of Arsenal.

4. **You'll have more friends.**

   True friends are found out when you play against the big boys. They call you out of the blue, tell you how nice you are and how well you've played in the Premiership and more importantly that they are free when you are playing against Man United or Arsenal. They think they are so kind volunteering coming to see a game and they want to discuss with you about Rooney or Gerrard. Didn't hear from them when we were playing Rotherham. They are 'Premiership friends'.

5. **You can't hide.**

   Every game, every small incident and feeling is widely reported and debated. There are too many cameras and eyes watching, no matter what you do, it can and will end up at the spotlight. A nasty tackle, a rude word, a great game or a skilful goal will not be unnoticed, they are all in the television, papers, radio, wherever you'll go, and you have to answer to it. There are no hidden corners, everything is found out and highlighted.

6. **Set pieces are extremely important.**

   Free-kicks, corners and penalties are key moments. When the margins are small, little things decide the winners. Open play and possession are unlikely to win you a game. But if you can bend it like Beckham you already have an advantage. The crucial points are won or lost at set pieces and by specialists of them.

7. **You can sometimes get Molton Brown body wash with your bath.**

   In the Championship you were lucky to get warm water and a toilet that didn't smell like last month's Chinese takeaway, but in the Premiership there can be luxuries you don't have at home. Stadiums, players, dressing rooms, car parks, shampoos, everything is bigger and better in the Premiership. You can smell the work of money everywhere.

8. **Don't give the ball away.**

   In the Premiership you have more time with the ball than other English divisions. The game is more European, based on possession and organisation. If you give the ball away there is every chance you won't see it for a long while. I think sometimes against teams like Arsenal you should play a multiball system: give another ball for the weaker team so they can also feel they're actually playing football.

9. **You get your name related to weird things.**

You live like in a constant Big Brother House, the camera is on all the time. Your name and life are public property. Whatever you've done or even tried is going to be noticed and published. Normally by whatever magazine for whatever reason. Just because I'm a blond foreigner writing for a paper, and an average Premiership player, I have been chosen for magazines; for example Top 100 Craziest Footballers of All Time, Starting XI of Gamblers, and Most Eligible Men from Finland. Why? I don't know.

10. **It is still football.**

Football can be played and seen in many different ways and levels. Still no matter what division or park game it is, the feelings, the rules and the starting score are still the same. You don't go out there thinking that you are a Premiership player. You go to play football. You play passionately and compete no matter what game it is. Because every game is competitive, fun and unpredictable. That is why it is the best sport in the world.

These are not the only things I've learned in the Premiership. Or the most important ones. Don't read them like the 10 Commandments, they are just what an average, blond Premiership player with a clamped car and too few points on the table has experienced in his season.

THE LAND WHERE THE JUMBLIES LIVE – 10 NONSENSICAL THOUGHTS FROM THE MADNESS OF SELHURST PARK

Riihilahti, of course, wrote the previous great, idiosyncratic list while playing for Crystal Palace. This is no coincidence: there must be something mysterious in the water that babbles through the brooks of London SE21, something that makes them talk the talk:

1. *The lad got over-excited when he saw the whites of the goal-post's eyes.*
   Crystal Palace manager, *Steve Coppell*

2. *I'm not going to make it a target, but it's something to aim for.*
   Coppell again

3. *I'm not going to drag it out or make a point, because points are pointless.*
   Crystal Palace chairman, *Simon Jordan*

4. *I made up a story about Alex Kolinko, who had been in tears after the game. I said he came from the poorest mountain village in Latvia where he had to fight bears when he was eight. I said his grandparents had been shot by the Nazis, his mother had died of cancer and his sister was raped by a gang of mountain rebels. But he never shed a single tear because he was strong and brave. Then I told them that one month playing behind our defence had turned him into a blubbering wreck! The players didn't know what to say. Except Clinton Morrison – he said, 'It's a shame about his sister.'*
   Crystal Palace manager, *Alan Smith*

5. *It's like one of those fairytales where you see a beautiful castle but when you get inside you discover years of decay. The princess, which is the players, is asleep. I'm trying to wake her, but it takes more than one kiss.*

   Smith again, warming to his themes of myth and fable ...

6. *It's a hard place to come for a southern team. You can dress well and have all the nice watches in the world, but that won't buy us a result at Grimsby.*

   ... and then coming down to earth with a bump as his team of daring marauders and sleeping beauties face the harsh reality of having to play a match in Cleethorpes.

7. *I was ordered to be babysitting the great Ali Bernabia. It's not my ideal football experience, but it is part of the job. It's so boring to follow for 90 minutes just one player, especially French-speaking.*

   Aki Riihilahti, the Palace and Finnish midfielder, describes the downside of the job as he's given a bum assignment against Manchester City's Algerian playmaker.

8. *Adrian attends Bromley Comprehensive and is a keen goalkeeper. In his spare time he likes listening to music and playing computer games. His favourite players have left the club.*

   Adrian, the pre-match mascot, files in his programme notes.

9. *I'm in* Miracle on 34th Street. *If you've seen the film, that's me. I believe in Father Christmas.*

   Manager **Iain Dowie** trying to stave off the inevitable with a frightening image.

10. *The big monster called relegation is there, ready to bite us on the arse.*

    Coppell, summing up the same situation in a more realistic, though nonetheless inventive way.

11 WORDS OF WISDOM

1. *When the dogs bark, the caravan just carries on through.*

   José Mourinho describes his new serenity in an expression translated from his native tongue. (Don't try saying that in Gillingham, José, it could all go a bit *Lock, Stock and Two Smoking Barrels.*)

This way please: José directs the caravan of love

2. *Some of our players have got no brains, so I've given them the day off tomorrow to rest them.*

   David Kemp, former Oxford United manager.

3. *Okay, so we lost, but good things can come from it – negative and positive.*

   Glenn Hoddle, torturing the logic.

4. *We pressed the self-destruct button ourselves.*

   Brian Kidd, former Blackburn manager, states the obvious.

5. *You weigh up the pros and cons and try to put them into chronological order.*

   Dave Bassett goes for the easy option; after all it's practically impossible to put them into phronhological order.

6. *I just felt that the whole night, the conditions, and taking everything into consideration, and everything being equal – and everything is equal – we should have got something from the game – but we didn't.*

   John Barnes, illustrating that sometimes it can feel the same being a player as it does being a fan.

7. *It's a conflict of parallels.*

   Sir Alex Ferguson, possibly expressing the same idea.

8. *The philosophy of a lot of European teams, even in home matches, is not to give a goal away.*

   Sir Alex again, offering an insight into the cunning ways of Johnny Foreigner.

9. *Very few of us have any idea whatsoever of what life is like living in a goldfish bowl – except, of course, for those of us who are goldfish.*

   Graham Taylor, being his peerless self.

10. *I was inbred into the game by my father.*

    David Pleat explains it all.

11. *We had enough chances to win this game. In fact, we did win.*

    It all turns out well in the end for Aberdeen manager, **Alex Smith**.

APOLLO XI

Ariel Ortega

Mark Venus   Sun Jihai   Jason Rockett   Adam Virgo

Phil Starbuck   Marc Overmars   Leo Fortune-West

Ramon Vega   Marco Stella   Tommy Mooney

MISCELLANEOUS
AT THE END OF THE JOUR, THEY THINK IT'S ALL OVER

THE RULES OF 5-A-SIDE

10 FISHY FACTS ABOUT GRIMSBY TOWN

4 ENGLAND CAPPED PLAYERS WHOSE
NAME ENDS WITH O

WORLD TEAMS OF THE TWENTIETH CENTURY:
EUROPEAN TEAM
SOUTH AMERICAN TEAM
WORLD TEAM

LAST WORDS

THE RULES OF 5-A-SIDE

Small-side football may be played with or without barriers. There is nothing in the laws that says the ball is only out if it goes past the tree in line with the corner of that building over there. In the interests of settling all future arguments, here are the rules in full.

1. **Playing Area**:
   Maximum Length: 140 feet (42.65 metres); Minimum Length: 85 feet (25.91 metres)
   Maximum Width: 85 feet (25.91 metres); Minimum Width: 55 feet (16.76 metres)

a) *Centre Mark*

A suitable mark should be made in the exact centre of the playing area 'on which the ball is dropped to commence a game. There is no rule that says the biggest loudmouth boots it into orbit to instigate play.

b) *Penalty Area*

A semi-circle of 25 feet (7.62 metres) radius shall be drawn from the centre of each goal line. The extremities of these semi-circles should reach the wall, touchlines or barricades regardless of whether or not the goalposts encroach onto the playing area.

Play Within the Penalty area:

Only the defending goalkeeper is allowed within the penalty area except when a penalty kick has been awarded, and then only the player taking the kick can enter the goal area. If a goalkeeper leaves the penalty area he is then treated as any other player.

Punishment for Infringement

(i) by the attack – a direct free kick at a point 6' (1.82 metres) outside the penalty area nearest to where the infringement occurred. You CANNOT score in the area. Everybody knows that.

(ii) by the defence – a penalty kick even if it *was* only accidental.

c) **Penalty Mark**

A penalty mark should be placed at a point 20 feet (6.09 metres) from the centre of each goal, though goalies are within their rights to pace it out at ten yards as this does seem a bit too close.

d) **Goal**

The goals shall be 16 feet (4.89 metres) long by 4 feet (1.21 metres) high or 12 feet (3.65 metres) long by 6 feet (1.82 metres) high. Otherwise they are from this crack to that crack on the garage wall this end, and between the tree and the traffic cone at the other end.

e) **Substitution Area**

Where barricades are not in use two substitution areas shall be marked 9 feet (2.74 metres) on each side of the halfway line (if one is marked) from which substitutions must be made. Each area will be 3 feet (0.91 metre) long and marked on the side line and will be 3 feet (0.91 metre) deep.

2. **Number of Players**

a) The match shall be played by two (2) teams. One (1)

player of each team shall be the goalkeeper, who must wear distinguishing colours.

b) Three (3) substitutes per team shall be permitted at any time during a game from a maximum of three (3) nominated substitutes.

c) The Rules of a Competition may allow for 'rolling' substitutes to be used. The number of 'rolling' substitutions is unlimited except in the case of the goalkeeper (see clause 2d).

A player who has been replaced may return to the playing area as a substitute for another player. A 'rolling' substitution is one which is made when the ball is still in play and is subject to the following conditions:

(i) the player leaving the playing area shall do so from the sideline crossing over at the substitution area.

(ii) the player entering the playing area shall do so from the substitution area but not until the player leaving the playing area has passed completely over the sideline.

(iii) where barricades are used a player must use the opening onto the playing area.

d) Any of the other players may change places with the goalkeeper, provided that the referee (?) is informed before the change is made, and provided also that the change is made during a stoppage in the game.

e) A match should not be considered valid if the playing strength of either team is reduced by more than two players. This rule may be disregarded by any team holding a winning advantage.

3. **Ball In and Out of Play**

   The ball shall be in play at all times from the start of the game unless:

a) the ball rises above 4' (1.21 metres) in the event of a height restriction being imposed;

b) the ball has crossed the goal-line, side-lines or the barricades surrounding the playing area or has landed on the garage roof.

c) the timekeeper, if appointed, has given the signal for half- or full-time. Watch? Anybody?

4. **The Ball**

   The ball will be supplied by the speccy kid, as that's the only way he gets a game.

5. **Players' Equipment**

a) Footwear shall be worn in accordance with the Laws of the Game, and subject to any local regulations.

b) The wearing of shinguards, which must be covered by stockings, in accordance with the Laws of the Game is compulsory. Any player who fails to wear shinguards does so at his or her own risk. No flipflops.

In short, and to sum up the above: it's Skins vs Shirts, you can have the speccy kid, last goal's the winner.

10
FISHY FACTS ABOUT GRIMSBY TOWN

An impostor haddock: actually a rainbow trout, as any fule kno

EVERY League has its club that will never be a Big Time Charlie, that plays at a ground like Blundell Park, a name that is a synonym for bleakness, a shed that no one in their right mind wants to visit. When a team is likely to be relegated in English football, their fans look at the table below and go, 'O shit we could be playing Crewe next year. O zut merde alors – and *Grimsby Town* too.'

1. They hold the highest attendance at Old Trafford: 76,962 for an FA Cup semi-final vs Wolves in 1939.

2. Used to give opposing teams fish.

3. Actually play in Cleethorpes.

4. Once managed by Bill Shankly.

5. In 1978 were unwilling to pay £30k for Gary Lineker.

6. Famous for the Brian Laws and Ivano Bonetti chicken incident*

7. In the '92/93 season, Newcastle United won their first 12 games, a run ended by Grimsby who beat them 1–0 at St James' Park.

8. The original Harry the Haddock inflatable mascot was actually a rainbow trout. †

9. Equal most promotions ever: 12.

10. Never ever played at Wembley ... until 1998 when they went twice in a month and won both times. (Play-off Final and Auto Windscreen Shield.)

*Ivano Bonetti was beloved of Grimsby fans for amazingly part-funding his own transfer to the club from Serie A. There came a point however when the Mariners boss Laws did not feel quite the same level of affection towards the ageing Italian. This was after a 3–2 defeat at Luton in 1996 when Laws concluded a post match discussion by throwing a plate of chicken wings at him. Skilful player though he was, Bonetti was unable to shift himself out of the way, caught the wings and plate full in the face, and hit the deck with a fractured cheekbone.

† *For readers without knowledge of Cleethorpes, Grimsby is a fishing port, famous for fish, a place where you might imagine that locals would be possessed of an educated ability to distinguish between one type of marine life and another.*

4 ENGLAND CAPPED PLAYERS WHOSE NAME ENDS WITH O

1. **John Atyeo** (Bristol City) 6 caps between 1956 and 1957

2. **Ken Shellito** (Chelsea) 1 cap in 1963

3. **John Salako** (Crystal Palace) 5 caps in 1991

4. **Tony Dorigo** (Chelsea, Leeds) 15 caps between 1990 and 1994

WORLD TEAMS OF THE TWENTIETH CENTURY

Released on June 10, 1998, in conjunction with the opening of the 1998 World Cup finals, the team was voted on by a panel that included 250 international soccer journalists. The panel selected European and South American Teams of the Century, and arrived at the World Team from those two lists:

Lev Yashin, greatest goalkeeper of all time

European Team

Lev Yashin
SOVIET UNION

Paolo Maldini   **Bobby Moore**   **Franz Beckenbauer**   **Franco Baresi**
ITALY   ENGLAND   WEST GERMANY   ITALY

Michel Platini   **Johan Cruyff**   **Eusebio**
FRANCE   NETHERLANDS   PORTUGAL

Marco Van Basten   **Ferenc Puskas**   **Bobby Charlton**
NETHERLANDS   HUNGARY   ENGLAND

South American Team

Ubaldo Fillol
ARGENTINA

Carlos Alberto
BRAZIL

Elias Figueroa
CHILE

Daniel Passarella
AGRENTINA

Nilton Santos
BRAZIL

Didi
BRAZIL

Alfredo Di Stefano
ARGENTINA

Rivelino
BRAZIL

Pele
BRAZIL

Garrincha
BRAZIL

Diego Maradona
ARGENTINA

World Team

Lev Yashin
SOVIET UNION

Carlos Alberto   **Bobby Moore**   **Franz Beckenbauer**   **Nilton Santos**
BRAZIL   ENGLAND   WEST GERMANY   BRAZIL

Michel Platini   **Alfredo Di Stefano**   **Johan Cruyff**
FRANCE   ARGENTINA   NETHERLANDS

Pele   **Garrincha**   **Diego Maradona**
BRAZIL   BRAZIL   ARGENTINA

LAST WORDS

1. Anybody who can do anything in Leicester but make a jumper has got to be a genius.
    Brian Clough *getting his local retaliation in while at the same time paying generous tribute to fellow manager Martin O'Neill.*

2. That's great: tell him he's Pele and get him back on.
    John Lambie, *as Partick Thistle manager, when told concussed striker Colin McGlashen did not know who he was.*

3. … and at number 11, Junior Bent, which I understand he is.
    Keith Valle, *the Bristol Rovers Tannoy announcer, at it again, as he concludes the team line-ups against deadly rivals Bristol City. He was fired for that, but later reinstated by popular demand.*

    A red rag to a bull for Keith Valle

4. Everybody was crying when we kept on winning and winning. So we draw at Goodison and that made people more happy and maybe gave them more hope. One day when we lose there will be a national holiday.
    José Mourinho, *dealing with Chelsea's role as the new Man United after their flying start (nine straight league wins) to the 2005/06 season.*

5. Football is a game – the language it don't matter as long as you run your bollocks off.
    Danny Bergara, *the Stockport County Uruguayan manager legend who dragged the team out of the basement, and to Wembley four times, but sadly always just missed out on that illustrious promotion to the old Second Division.*

6. As one door closes, another one shuts.
   ***Howard Wilkinson**, Leeds manager.*

7. At the end of Wilkinson's team talks we all be thinking: 'Eh?'
   ***David Batty**, player under Wilkinson.*

8. One minute you can be riding the crest of a wave in this game and the next minute you can be down. It's a great leveller and you can't get too cock-a-hoop about things. I know it's an old cliché but you've got to take each game as it comes and keep working at it. Whether you're playing or in management, you're only as good as your last game.
   ***Billy Bonds**, as manager of West Ham in the early '90s. You somehow suspect that when his team wins, Billy is over the moon.*

9. One day I'm going to answer the phone and someone will say, 'Harry, we're eighth in the league with a good squad, and youngsters coming through. We're doing all right, but the manager has just left for Real Madrid and we need someone to take us to the next stage.' I never get that, I get, 'Harry, we're in the cart.' That will be my epitaph: here lies Harry Bassett. Deep in the shit, where he started.
   ***Harry Bassett**, manager of many struggling teams.*

10. Here I am, tear me limb from limb.
    ***Gordon McKeag**, Newcastle Chairman, to reporters after relegation in 1989.*

THE WORLD CUP
EL MUNDIAL, LA COPPA DEL MONDO, DIE FUSSBALLWELTMEISTERSCHAFT, LA COUPE DU MONDE

THE WINNERS

1966 Winners

Year	Winner	Score	Runner-up	Host
1930	Uruguay	4–2	Argentina	Uruguay
1934	Italy	2–1	Czechoslovakia	Italy
1938	Italy	4–2	Hungary	France
1950	Uruguay	2–1	Brazil	Brazil
1954	Germany	3–2	Hungary	Switzerland
1958	Brazil	5–2	Sweden	Sweden
1962	Brazil	3–1	Czechoslovakia	Chile
1966	England	4–2	Germany	England
1970	Brazil	4–1	Italy	Mexico
1974	Germany	2–1	Netherlands	Germany
1978	Argentina	3–1	Netherlands	Argentina
1982	Italy	3–1	Germany	Spain
1986	Argentina	3–2	Germany	Mexico
1990	Germany	1–0	Argentina	Italy
1994	Brazil	3–2	Italy (on pens)	USA
1998	France	3–0	Brazil	France
2002	Brazil	0–2	Germany	Japan/Korea

THE 7 COUNTRIES WHO HAVE WON

Country	Won	When
Brazil	5	1958, 1962, 1970, 1994, 2002
Italy	3	1934, 1938, 1982
Germany	3	1954, 1974, 1990
Uruguay	2	1930, 1950
Argentina	2	1978, 1986
England	2	1966
France	1	1998

10 REASONS WHY THE WORLD CUP IS GREAT

1. The anticipation.

2. Queueing to get into a pub at 7 a.m. to watch a game, ending up dancing in a Chinese restaurant at midnight with no idea what the result was or who you are.

3. Learning the names of star players for Latvia/Senegal/ Iran/South Korea/Togo.

4. Penalty shoot-outs.

5. Brazilian female fans in bikinis.

6. Three matches in one day during the group stages so you never have to leave your living room.

7. Watching footage of every Spanish person in the world drive around for 24 hours beeping their horns and waving their flags and setting off fireworks after a quarter-final victory before the inevitable happens in the semi.

8. Seeing the player you've never heard of who produced the odd moment of genius get signed by a Premiership club for a ludicrous amount of money and then turn out to be the poor man's Thomas Brolin.

9. Impromptu 5-a-side matches in the local park vs foreign students.

10. Showing off your Cruyff turn in impromptu 5-a-sides vs foreign students.

10 REASONS WHY THE WORLD CUP IS CRAP

1. Opening ceremony with Diana Ross or similar 'Superstar soccer fan' singing terrible song and missing penalty with only a mascot, who isn't even trying to save it, to beat.

2. The Mexican Wave.

3. Facepaint.

4. Excuses for failure:
   i) It was too hot
   ii) We need a mid-season break
   iii) The biased referee

5. Panini World Cup stickers (there's nobody in the world who needs or wants 57 Gary Nevilles)

Robert Baggio's missed spot kick gifts the trophy to Brazil, World Cup 1994

6. Great Escape ringtones.

7. Penalty shoot-outs.

8. Maracas and other percussion instruments.

9. Scottish people wearing Brazil/Argentina/whoever-England-are-playing shirts. How sad.

10. Going to casualty with ruptured ankle ligaments after showing off your Cruyff turn in impromptu 5-a-sides vs foreign students.

PLANET WORLD CUP'S TOP 10 TEAMS

1. Brazil 1970

Often described as the best football team of all time. It had individual world-class players overall in midfield and attack. Pele, Jairzinho, Tostao, Rivelino, the list goes on and on. They won all their six games in the Cup of 1970.

2. West Germany 1974

This was also a superb team. Beckenbauer as leader in defence and behind him was Sepp Maier, one of the best goalkeepers of all time. Overath and Bonhof were also quality players and of course the notorious Gerd Müller up front, who averaged more than a goal a game for the Germans, and scored the winning goal in the final itself.

3. Italy 1982

They started the tournament with three draws, but then found form and beat Argentina, Brazil, Poland and West Germany in consecutive matches. They based their team on defensive strength. Forty-year-old Dino Zoff was the captain and goalkeeper and he had Gentile and Scirea as leaders in defence. Dangerous winger Bruno Conti was instrumental as well as midfielder Tardelli. Up front was Paolo Rossi in top form as the tournament progressed, and scored six times in Italy's last three matches.

4. **Brazil 1994**

Brazil had in 1994 for once a solid defence, and that was the main reason why, for the first time in 24 years, they managed to win the World Cup. Romario was their outstanding player, and he had Bebeto as colleague up front. Other great players were Leonardo, Dunga and Jorginho.

5. **Holland 1974**

Holland 1974: had all the qualities

They didn't win the World Cup, but they still deserve a place on the Top 10 list of great teams. They scored 15 goals in the Cup and only let in one goal on their way to the final and that was an own goal. Cruyff, Neeskens, Rep, Rensenbrink and van Hanegem thrilled the world, and could with a little more luck have won the Cup. They had all the qualities.

6. **West Germany 1990**

   Definitely a worthy champion of the dull tournament in Italy in 1990. They were one of the very few teams who relied on attacking skills rather than defensive safety, and were rewarded with the Cup. Matthäus was their great player, alongside attacking left-back Brehme who scored the winning goal in the final itself. Other great names were Klinsmann, Völler and Kohler.

7. **France 1998**

   The winners had their strength in a central line with Blanc and Desailly in defence to Petit and Deschamp in midfield. The team was built around those players. Attacking full-backs Lizarazu and Thuram helped in attack as France lacked world-class strikers. This was tactically a very strong team.

8. **Hungary 1954**

   Another team who failed to win the Cup, but had all the qualities. Scored an incredible 27 goals in the 1954 Cup. They beat both Brazil and defending champions Uruguay 4–2, but lost 3–2 in the final to West Germany. This team had legends like Puskas, Kocsis and Hidegkuti and hadn't lost in 30 games before the final, until Brazil in 2002.

9. **Argentina 1986**

   This team of course had Maradona and that made them automatically a great team. But other players contributed as well, among them were Burruchaga, Valdano and the great centre-back Ruggeri. They helped Argentina win the Cup in 1986. This team was also the last team so far to become champions without needing extra-time or penalty shoot-outs on their way, until Brazil in 2002.

10. **Brazil 1958**

This class of '58 invented the famous 4–2–4 system. It also saw Pele emerge as a 17-year-old, having started the tournament on the bench. Garrincha, Vava, Didi and Zagallo were other famous names in Brazil's first ever World Cup triumph.

There are so many great teams we also would have liked to see on the list, but didn't quite make it. For instance, the great Brazilian team of 1982. But when you can't get past the second phase, do you really deserve a place on the Top 10 ranking of all time? Lots of quality players in midfield and attack, but the defence was unstable to say the least.

Another team in contention was Italy of 1990. In many ways the counterpart of the Brazilian team just mentioned. They kept a clean sheet until the semi-final, but didn't quite have the edge in attack to win tournaments. Schillaci was virtually the only offensive player who was shining.

Uruguay had teams who won the World Cup, but because it's now half a century since they won, we decided not to add them. The game has changed a lot, but we still respect and rate them highly. England of 1966 also was a team we debated over, but suffered the same fate as Argentina in 1978. They used the home advantage to a high degree of efficiency in years when heavyweights like Brazil, Italy and West Germany were rebuilding for the future and appeared with some of their weaker teams.

Reproduced with the kind permission of the excellent website www.planetworldcup.com.

5 VALUABLE ITEMS OF MEMORABILIA

1. Yellow Brazil shirt worn by Pele in the 1970 World Cup final.

   The hammer finally fell at Christies at £157,750, a record for a football shirt at auction.

2. Alan Ball's England 1966 World Cup Final medal.

   Sold for £164,800 in 2005.

3. Gordon Banks'* World Cup Final medal.

   Fetched £124,000 in 2001.

4. Red England shirt worn by Geoff Hurst in the 1966 World Cup Final.

   Sold for £91,750 in 2000.

5. Alan Ball's England 1966 World Cup tournament cap.

   Sold for £43,200 in 2005.

* Regarded by many as England's greatest 'keeper, Banks lost an eye in a car accident in 1972. Such was his stature that the BBC interrupted its programmes for news flashes. In his period of recovery, his then manager at Stoke City, Tony Waddington, believing that his 'keeper was so outstanding that he could continue to play even given this disability, spent time after training popping shots at him from all angles. This exercise convinced him that for all his brilliance, even Banksy really could not carry on with the loss of peripheral vision his injury entailed.

11 MASCOTS

The World Cup mascot was introduced to the 1966 tournament in England, when a man dressed in a lion suit did stuff round the perimeter of the track at Wembley. From then on, each World Cup has had one (or two, as in 1974, or three, as in 2002). They have been popular symbols, and millions of people have bought copies of them, so we're told. The ground rule seems to be that whatever form the mascot takes, it must always be happy and smiley.

1. **England 1966**   *World Cup Willie* – a happy football-playing lion.
2. **Mexico 1970**   *Juanito* – a happy little boy.
3. **West Germany 1974**   *Tip & Tap* – two happy little boys.
4. **Argentina 1978**   *Gauchito* – a happy little boy.
5. **Spain 1982**   *Naranjito* – a smiling orange.
6. **Mexico 1986**   *Pique* – a happy chilli pepper.
7. **Italy 1990**   *Ciao* – not easy to tell what this is. Some kind of happy Lego sculpture?
8. **United States 1994**   *Striker* – a smiling dog.
9. **France 1998**   *Footix* – a smiling cockerel.
10. **Korea/Japan 2002**   *Kaz, Ato and Nik* – three charming happy, funny creatures.
11. **Germany 2006**   *GOLEO VI* – a happy, cheeky lion.

HALF A DOZEN DUALISTS: PLAYERS WHO HAVE APPEARED FOR 2 NATIONS

The rules are changed now, and no player will ever be playing for more than one country again. Gifted playmaker Deco, star of Porto's brilliant 2004 Champions League campaign, was born in Brazil but accepted an offer to play for Portugal, where he has played since 1998.

Player	Nations	Caps
1. *Luisito Monti* *	Argentina (1924–1931)	16
	Italy (1932–1936)	18
2. *Ferenc Puskas*	Hungary (1945–1956)	85
	Spain (1961–1962)	4
3. *Alfredo Di Stéfano*	Argentina (1947)	6
	Spain (1957–1961)	31
4. *José Santamaria*	Uruguay (1952–1957)	20
	Spain (1958–1962)	16
5. *José João Altafini*	Brazil (1957–1958)	8
(aka Mazzola)	Italy (1961–1962)	6
6. *Robert Prosinecki*	Yugoslavia (1989–1990)	15
	Croatia (1993–2002)	49

Monti was not altogether a gentleman: Chelsea toured South America in the late 1920s, and in a fixture against Boca Juniors Monti was reported to have offered his hand to the left half in a gesture that appeared to be one of friendship. When the player offered his own hand, Monti kicked him.

THE 6 FASTEST GOALS

Player	Match	Time (seconds)	Tournament
Hakan Sükür	**Turkey** 3–2 South Korea	11	2002 Korea/ Japan
Vaclav Masek	**Czechoslovakia** 1–3 Mexico	15	1962 Chile
Park Soong-Jin	**North Korea** 3–5 Portugal	23	1966 England
Ernst Lehner	**Germany** 3–2 Austria	24	1934 Italy
Bryan Robson	**England** 3–1 France	27	1982 Spain
Bernard Lacombe	**France** 1–2 Italy	37	1978 Argentina

1 FASTEST SUPER-SUB GOAL

| Ebbe Sand | **Denmark** 4–1 Nigeria | 16 | 1998 France |

Scored in the 60th minute, 16 seconds after coming on, Sand's is the fastest goal by a substitute.

MOST DEADLY SCORERS

Goals	Player	Nationality	Tournaments
14	Gerd Müller	GER	(1970, '74)
13	Just Fontaine★	FRA	(1958)
12	Pele	BRA	(1958, '62, '66, '70)
11	Sándor Kocsis	HUN	(1954)
	Jürgen Klinsmann	GER	(1990, '94, '98)
10	Helmut Rahn	GER	(1954, '58)
	Teófilo Cubillas	PER	(1970, '78)
	Lato Grzegorz	POL	(1974, '78, '82)
	Gary Lineker	ENG	(1986, '90)
9	Vavá	BRA	(1958, '62)
	Eusébio	POR	(1966)
	Jairzinho	BRA	(1966, '70)
	Uwe Seeler	GER	(1958, '62, '66, '70)
	Paolo Rossi	ITA	(1978, '82, '86)
	K.H. Rummenige	GER	(1978, '82, '86)
	Roberto Baggio	ITA	(1990, '94, '98)
	Gabriel Batistuta	ARG	(1994, '98)
8	Guillermo Stábile	ARG	(1930)
	Leônidas	BRA	(1934, '38)
	Oscar Míguez	URU	(1950, '54)
	Diego Maradona	ARG	(1982, '86, '90, '94)
	Rudi Völler	GER	(1986, '90, '94)
7	Ademir	BRA	(1950)
	Hans Schäfer	GER	(1954, '58)
	Lajos Tichy	HUN	(1958, '62)
	Johnny Rep	HOL	(1974, '78)
	Andrzej Szarmach	POL	(1974, '78, '82)
	Careca	BRA	(1986, '90)

★ *See panel on next page.*

JUST FONTAINE – FRENCH GOALSCORING LEGEND

France Football magazine named Just Fontaine as the fifth-best French player of all time, behind Michel Platini, Zinedine Zidane, Raymond Kopa and Laurent Blanc. But Just is best-known as the holder of a World Cup record that is unlikely to be broken. At the 1958 finals in Sweden he scored in all six games, notching up an unprecedented 13 goals. Over 45 years later, the French striker's record still stands as the highest of any player in a single World Cup. The achievement is made more noteworthy because Fontaine had been lucky to get a game in the national side at all until his Reims teammate René Bliard was ruled out with an ankle injury. It was as a consequence of this that Fontaine was given his chance. He formed a prolific partnership with Kopa which took a France side that had not won all year to 3rd place in the tournament.

Fontaine announced his arrival on the World Cup stage with a hat-trick as France thrashed Paraguay 7–3. In the next three group games, he bagged another five against Yugoslavia, Scotland and Northern Ireland, to set up a semi-final meeting with eventual winners Brazil. Fontaine scored one to take his tournament total to nine, but it wasn't enough as Brazil triumphed 5–2, and a teenage superstar took centre stage – the difference between the two teams could be summed up in one word: Pele. Undeterred, Fontaine commiserated in the best possible way by scoring four against West Germany in the third place play-off. Fontaine says:

There wasn't a Golden Boot award or anything like that in 1958, so no one thought about it. That probably gave me an advantage. Nowadays, as soon as a striker scores three goals, everyone starts asking him about it. As soon as he thinks about the record, he's finished. The secret is to put it out of your mind. In those days there was not so much pressure on us. Only two journalists followed the team around. Our team bosses were so convinced we would be knocked out that they only gave us three shirts each, so we were totally free from pressure. My mind was not on the goals record at all. I even turned down the chance to take a penalty in the third-place game! Teams are less attacking now. To beat my record, a side would really have to go for it, or a player would need to go on a goal spree in the group matches. Because the group games are like a mini-tournament, teams tend to be very calculating, so it becomes very difficult.

Fontaine also holds a much less coveted record – he was in charge of the French national team in 1967 for two games, on 22 March and 3 June: the shortest reign anyone has had as manager of France.

THE MOST GOALS IN 1 MATCH

5 – Oleg Salenko (RUS) vs Cameroon in 1994

4 – Emilio Butragueño (SPA) vs Denmark in 1986

4 – Eusebio (POR) vs North Korea in 1966

4 – Just Fontaine (FRA) vs West Germany in 1958

4 – Sandor Kocsis (HUN) vs West Germany in 1954

4 – Ademir (BRA) vs Sweden in 1950

4 – Juan Schiaffino (URU) vs Bolivia in 1950

4 – Leônidas (BRA) vs Poland in 1938

4 – Ernst Willimowski (POL) vs Brazil in 1938

4 – Gustav Wetterström (SWE) vs Cuba in 1938

11 HAT-TRICKS

1. **Bert Patenaude**

   The first player to score a hat-trick in a World Cup match was United States star Patenaude, against Paraguay in the first round of the 1930 World Cup. FIFA do not record it, having him down for just two goals, but his teammates said he scored all three.

2. **Laszlo Kiss**

   The fastest hat-trick was made by Hungary's Laszlo Kiss against El Salvador in 1982, when he scored after 70, 74 and 77 minutes. Kiss is also the only substitute to have scored a hat-trick.

3. **Paolo Rossi**

   A suspension for a bribe scandal saw the player out of action for two years. But just weeks before the 1982

World Cup, coach Enzo Bearzot selected Rossi for the World Cup despite his having played only a few times in the preceding couple of seasons. He played four games without scoring, and the pressure on player and manager was intense, with calls for Rossi to be dropped. But in the quarter-final match against favourites Brazil, he scored a hat-trick and sent Italy to the semis, where he scored both goals in the 2–0 win against Poland. He scored the opener in Italy's 3–1 victory over West Germany in the final. Those six goals made him top scorer of the tournament. Afterwards, his face was on every billboard in Italy, where he could be seen endorsing everything from sunglasses to yoghurt.

4. **Sándor Kocsis**

Double hat-trick. Hungary's Kocsis was the first player to score consecutive hat-tricks. they took place in the four days covering 17 June 1954, vs Korea, and 20 June 1954, vs Germany.

5. **Gerd Müller**

Another double hat-trick. Müller's were the only hat-tricks of the 1970 finals, coming against Bulgaria and Peru. His three against Bulgaria were notable in that he scored in three different ways: from open play with his boot, with a header, and from the penalty spot.

6. **Gabriel Batistuta**

The Argentinian is the only player to score hat-tricks in two separate tournaments, each time with the help of a penalty, each time against the weakest team in the group. His first hat-trick against Greece in 1994 were his first goals in any World Cup finals. His second was in 1998 against Jamaica.

7. **Harry Andersson**

   A debut hat-trick: Andersson scored a hat-trick on his International debut for Sweden against Cuba in 1938.

8. **Ernst Willimowski**

   Poland 5–6 Brazil (1938). Poor Willimowski scored a hat-trick plus one, the last being his fourth in extra time, and still ended up on the losing side. He appears to have been the only player to achieve this unhappy distinction in any official senior international match.

9. **Oleg Salenko**

   The only player ever to score a hat-trick plus two, netting five times in the 1994 game between Russia and Cameroon. It took him 59 minutes.

10. **Geoff Hurst**

    Possibly the most famous hat-trick in footballing history: Hurst became the first – and to date only – player to score three in a World Cup final, in 1966. He took 102 minutes to score three goals, including the famous 'did it cross the line?' goal.

11. **Pele**

    The youngest hat-trick scorer, against France in the semi-final in Sweden, 1958.

King of the superlatives, Pele: the youngest hat-trick scorer, 1958

11 DISCIPLINARY MATTERS

1. **The first player ever to be sent off in a World Cup match**

   Was Peru's *Mario de Las Casas* against Romania in 1930.

2. **First player to be sent off in a World Cup final**

   Pedro Monzon of Argentina achieved this record in the final against West Germany in Rome in 1990. His teammate *Gustavo Dezotti* also received a red card later in the same match. *Marcel Desailly* of France is the only other player to have been sent off in a final, against Brazil in 1998.

3. **First red card**

   The opening game of the 1970 World Cup at the Azteca Stadium between Mexico and the Soviet Union marked the start of a new era as substitutions and red and yellow cards were used for the first time in the competition's history. Rated by many as the best World Cup ever, 1970 was an exceptionally clean tournament with not a single dismissal: Chile's *Carlos Caszely*, in a match against West Germany in 1974, was the first player to be shown the red card.

4. **First yellow card**

   Lovchev of the Soviet Union did at least manage to get his name in the book in that opening match at the Azteca in 1970.

5. **Fastest red card**

   José Batista of Uruguay was sent off after just 56 seconds against Scotland in 1986. That is the earliest early bath in World Cup history, his foul on *Gordon Strachan* giving French referee *Joël Quiniou* little option. Scotland followers will have painful memories of the 10 men of Uruguay keeping the score goalless for the remaining 89 minutes, and progressing to the next round at the expense of 'Ally's Army'.

6. **Fastest red card to a substitute**

Bolivia's *Marco Etcheverry* was sent off after three minutes on the field as a substitute in the match against Germany in Soldier Field, Chicago, 1994.

7. **The Rob Styles award**

The most card-happy ref in World Cup history is *Arturo Brizio Carter* of Mexico, who sent off seven players in the six games he was in charge of between 1994 and 1998.

8. **One exceptional booking**

Ramon Quiroga was 'keeper for Peru in the 1978 World Cup. He was similar to his Colombian colleague René Higuita in his flamboyant style of goalkeeping. In the dying stages of Peru's match against Poland, Ramon distinguished himself by being the only 'keeper to be booked for a foul in the opponent's half of the field.

9. **The only player to be sent off in successive tournaments**

The player raising his arms in the air in the traditional mime of innocence and disbelief is *Mr Rigobert Song*. The Cameroonian player received his marching orders against Brazil in 1994 and again against Chile in 1998.

10. David Beckham

The whole world remembers Beckham's flick at Diego Simeone during the match of the tournament at France '98: the ensuing brouhaha was all a part of the hysteria that raised the player to a global phenomenon. Beckham gained a huge measure of revenge by scoring from the spot to help knock out Argentina in 2002. He had to cope with Simeone trying to shake his hand before the kick, and he knew the consequences of missing would be immense. His subsequent arms-wide celebration said it all.

11. First goalkeeper sent off

Gianluca Pagliuca of Italy got his dues against Norway in 1994 for handling outside his area, though everybody knows that this category ought rightly to belong to *Toni Schumacher*. The German 'keeper should have been locked up, never mind sent off, for his attempt to decapitate *Patrick Battiston* in the semi-final between Germany and France in 1982, whereas, for reasons only a referee could know, Dutch official Charles Corver failed to sanction Schumacher or even award France a free-kick.

WORLD CUP TRIVIA TOP 20

1. No **host** country has ever been eliminated in the first round.

2. Erik Nilsson of Sweden and Alfred Bickel of Switzerland are the only men to have played in the World Cup **either**

side of World War II. They each appeared in the 1938 and 1950 tournaments.

3. The **youngest** player to have appeared in a World Cup match was Norman Whiteside of Northern Ireland in 1982. He was 17 years and 42 days old when he played against Yugoslavia.

4. For the United Arab Emirates, qualifying for Italia '90 was a first and an achievement in itself. The UEA were knocked out after three straight defeats in the group stage. However, they managed to score two goals (one in a 1–5 defeat by Germany, one in a 1–4 defeat by Yugoslavia), and the goal scorers – Khalid Ismail Mubarak and Ali Thani Jumaa – celebrated as if they had won the World Cup. No wonder: the players received the **gift** of a Rolls Royce for every goal they scored.

5. The **heaviest defeat** ever inflicted was by Hungary over El Salvador in Spain, 1982. In this game Laszlo Kiss of Hungary became the only substitute to score a hat-trick in the World Cup. Hungary were already 5–1 up when Kiss scored his first of three in this match against. The game ended 10–1 which is the **biggest victory** in World Cup history.

6. Mario Zagallo managed Brazil to their 1970 triumph in Mexico. With that he became the first man to **play** in and go on to **manage** a World Cup winning team. He was a member of the Brazilian sides which won the trophy in 1958 and 1962.

Later *Franz Beckenbauer* emulated the feat, lifting the World Cup as captain of Germany in 1974 and repeating the accomplishment as manager in 1990.

7. Sweden have played Brazil **seven** times in World Cup history. No other countries have met more often.

8. The **most capped** player at the World Cup finals is Lothar Matthäus of Germany with **25** games. His greatest year was 1990 when Germany won the final in Rome and Matthäus was also voted European Player of the Year and Player of the Year in Germany as well.

9. Usually the World Cup final produces goals. No final match had produced fewer than three untilWest Germany beat Argentina by 1–0 in 1990. That winning goal was scored from the penalty spot by Andreas Brehme, and with the 1994 final ending in a penalty shoot-out after a goalless draw, it meant that Jorge Burruchaga's winner for Argentina against West Germany in the 1986 final was the last goal **not** scored from the **penalty spot** in a World Cup final until 2000, when France beat Brazil in Paris.

10. Girly long-haired players and fairies with earrings did not have a future in the Argentine national side as long as Daniel Passarella was the coach. He set strict appearance rules for the candidates to the tournament in France 1998. After protracted media posturing, even Gabriel Batistuta finally went to the salon for a **trim** in order not to miss out on the World Cup.

11. The International Network of Street Papers organise the **Homeless** World Cup, where teams made up entirely of homeless people compete. The INSP hopes to use the positive effect of football to highlight the issues of global poverty and homelessness, as well as to use the sport as a social integrator for its participants. The event is held

annually. The first Homeless World Cup took place in July 2003 in Austria. Ironically, Austria, seizing home advantage, went on to win the tournament.

12. The most goals scored in one match is **12**: Austria 7–5 Switzerland in 1954.

13. The Italians have no serious competition when it comes to throwing their toys out of the pram and are the biggest World Cup **cry babies**. North Korea sent Italy out of the 1966 World Cup in the group stage. In Italy such an early exit is not acceptable. The team flight home had a secret destination to avoid the press, media and angry fans. But many supporters still found out where they were arriving, and their bus at the airport was bombarded by fruit and rotten tomatoes as they escaped. In an echo to this, North Korea's neighbours in the south achieved a memorable victory over the Azzuri in the tournament they co-hosted with Japan, in 2002. In the first knock-out round, South Korea beat Italy 2–1 by a golden goal, Italy, down to 10 men, finally falling to a 117th-minute header from *Ahn Jung-Hwan.* Jung-Hwan played his club football in Italy, for Perugia. Perugia's president Luciano Gaucci banned Jung-Hwan from coming back to play for the club! Gaucci said he would no longer employ Ahn, claiming that his club's decision was prompted not by his goal but by his remarks afterwards, which were, *Offensive to me and the whole Italian nation* '... Ahn said Korean football was superior to Italian football, when Italy is a footballing nation. We have treated him well with all our love, but his comments were offensive to me and to the whole Italian nation. That gentleman will never set foot in Perugia again. He was a phenomenon only when he

played against Italy. I am a nationalist and I regard such behaviour not only as an affront to Italian pride but also an offence to a country which two years ago opened its doors to him. I have no intention of paying a salary to someone who has ruined Italian soccer.'

So there.

14. Frenchman Michel Vautrot allowed eight minutes of **added time** in the first period of extra-time in the semi-final between Italy and Argentina in 1990. He later admitted he forgot about the clock.

15. No **captain** has held the World Cup aloft more than once. Diego Maradona of Argentina and Dunga of Brazil have come closest. Maradona captained Argentina to victory in 1986 and to the silver medal in 1990. Dunga won as captain in 1994 and lost the final in 1998. Karl-Heinz Rummenigge is the only captain to lose two World Cup finals – 1982 and 1986.

16. The longest unbeaten sequence in World Cup history belongs to goalkeeper **Walter Zenga**. The Italian 'keeper played for 517 minutes (nearly 6 games) without letting in a goal in 1990. Claudio Caniggia of Argentina ended his run, scoring in open play in a 1–1 draw in the semi-final. Italy lost on penalties. The most finals matches played by a goalkeeper without conceding a goal is the 10 achieved by **Peter Shilton** of England from 1982 to 1990.

17. The unenvied record of most games without a win belongs to Bulgaria, who went on a sequence of **17** winless matches in the tournaments: 1962–1974, 1986 and 1994. They finally put the hex to rest by beating Greece 4–0 in Chicago.

18. The Brazilian Carlos Alberto Parreira has coached **four** different **countries**: Kuwait '82, United Arab Emirates '90, Brazil '94 (Champions) and Saudi Arabia '98.

19. The **oldest** player to have won the World Cup is Dino Zoff of Italy. He was 40 years old when he captained Italy to victory in 1982. Roger Milla is the tournament's oldest goal-scorer, netting the consolation goal in Cameroon's 6–1 defeat at the hands of Russia at the age of 42 years and 39 days. Leslie Compton was the oldest player to make his debut for England, at 38.

20. The **youngest** player to have won the World Cup is **Pele**. He was 17 years and 249 days old when Brazil beat Sweden 5–2 in the 1958 final.

CONTRIBUTORS

Trezza Azzopardi is a Booker-listed novelist. She knows very little about football, as she grew up in Wales.

Edward Banks is a staunch Norwich City supporter who occasionally writes to the *Eastern Daily Press* on NCFC-related matters.

Paul Bennett works in television and film as a third assistant director. He has managed to convince many American celebrities that Coventry City are the best team in England.

Stuart Butler is founder of the football poets (www.footballpoets.org), ex-Swindon Boys FC, and is about to undertake professional training for secondary school headship. He is the owner of Basil the Westie, who caused quite a stir when the FA turned him down as prospective England manager and chose Sven-Göran Eriksson instead.

Stuart Cosgrove is the author of *Hampden Bablyon – The History of Sex and Scandal in Scottish Football*, and works for Channel 4.

Mark Eltringham is a journalist when he wants to be, but can also don a suit when he wants people to think he's a marketing consultant, which pays more. After selling out in this way, he tries to maintain his credibility by refusing to wear ties or get a decent haircut.

Magnus Eriksson lives in the Swedish city of Lund. He follows Östers IF, the Swedish and English national sides and Tottenham Hotspur. He is a keen whisky drinker who writes about literature, music and American issues for the eminent Stockholm newspaper, *Svenska Dagbladet*.

Patricia Gregory was one of the founders of the Women's FA in the late 1960s. She was a player and referee, and ran a club, league and the Association in an honorary capacity until the 1990s. She served on the UEFA Women's Football Committee for 14 years as well as being a member of the FA Women's Football Committee. Earning a living sometimes seemed to be her spare-time occupation (35 years in sports broadcasting and still going strong).

Benedict Paul Gerard Vincent Keane is a hack provincial lawyer whose likes include eating offal and being contrary. His dislikes are too numerous to mention but revolve around anybody having the gall to hold similar ideals and values to his own.

Anjali Pratap was born in Plumstead, which means she should support Palace or Charlton. But her boyfriend is a lifelong follower of Spurs, ergo, it's a no-brainer.

Andy Smith is an AFC Bournemouth fan whose record-filing system is so confused that Graham Coxon comes under C while Ian Brown is under I. His previous forays into the world of literature include contributing to a book commemorating the last days of Dean Court and once having a letter published in *When Saturday Comes*.

John Street teaches politics at the University of East Anglia and is the author of books on mass media and popular culture. He plays hockey when he should be watching football, but at least he has been sent off a few times.

George Szirtes came to England as a refugee in 1956. He has written some 20-odd books never once mentioning Manchester United. He latest collection, *Reel* (Bloodaxe, 2004), won the TS Eliot Prize. He didn't mention United there either, but love will out.

INDEX

INDEX

INDEX